Sunset

An Illustrated Guide to
Attracting Birds

By the Editors of Sunset Books and Sunset Magazine

Painted bunting (see page 52)

Sunset Publishing Corporation ▪ Menlo Park, California

Black-capped chickadee

Barn swallow

Book Editor
Susan Warton

Research & Text
Daniel P. Murphy
Kit and George Harrison
Philip Edinger
Scott Atkinson

Coordinating Editor
Suzanne Normand Mathison

Design
Joe di Chiarro

Illustrations
Lois Lovejoy
Bill Oetinger

Maps
Eureka Cartography

Cover: Black-capped chickadee. Photography: Mary Clay/Tom Stack & Associates. *Special CD-ROM version:* Mourning dove. Photography: Glenn Christiansen. Design: Susan Bryant.

Editorial Director, Sunset Books: Kenneth Winchester

Seventh printing April 1995

Baltimore oriole

"Drink your teeeeee. . ."

. . . chides a rufous-sided towhee. "Dzrrt" calls the eastern meadowlark. "Gerald-deeeen" peals a wood thrush. And a flock of foraging bushtits chatters "tsit-tsit-tsit."

In a garden that attracts birds, these and similar songs and calls fill the air with natural music. Birds also bring beauty, color, astonishing flight patterns, and fascinating drama to the world outside the window or off the patio.

Sunset has published previous books on birds. We brought out our *Introduction to Western Birds* as long ago as 1953. *Attracting Birds to Your Garden,* a respected resource in the birding community, was published in 1974.

Now we introduce this entirely new title celebrating the joys of backyard bird-watching. In the first chapter, you'll discover the distinctive characteristics of birds and learn how to identify them. The next chapter features an easy-to-use field guide to 80 birds that frequently visit North American gardens; each entry is accompanied by a range map and full-color photograph.

Creating a bird-welcoming habitat is the focus of the third chapter, where you'll find seasoned advice and recommendations for plants that will attract birds. The final chapters explain how to provide your feathered guests with supplemental food, water, and shelter. You'll learn everything from how to make a suet cake to how to build your own purple martin apartment.

Enriching the book from cover to cover are colorful photographs and illustrations of birds, as well as maps of species ranges and garden climate zones.

We are grateful to the following individuals and organizations for their expert assistance with the text, photographs, maps, and artwork: Richard W. Stallcup; Peter J. Metropulos; G. Denny Mallory; Richard Clarke, The Bird House; National Geographic Society; Ted Chandik; Peter La Tourrette, Bay Area Bird Photographers; Karen Sullivan, Hummingbird Gardens Nursery; Cliff Richer, Sequoia Audubon Society; Lynn Tennefoss, Santa Clara Valley Audubon Society; National Wildlife Federation; National Audubon Society; U.S. Fish & Wildlife Service, Department of the Interior; Ray Peterson; Richardson Bay Audubon Society; Golden Gate Audubon Society; Bushnell Division of Bausch & Lomb; Astronomics/Christophers Ltd.; Leica USA Inc.; Wild Bird Co.; Wild Bird Supplies; Audubon Workshop; Bird 'n Hand Inc.; Droll Yankees, Inc.; Duncraft; Hyde Bird Feeder Co.; Menlo Park Hardware Co.; The Nature Company; Smith & Hawken; The Dick E. Bird News.

Special thanks go to Phyllis Elving for carefully editing the manuscript.

White-breasted nuthatch

House finch

Contents

Indigo bunting

Yellow warbler

Mourning dove

LOOK! An Indigo Bunting

*L*ook up—see more than a hundred pine siskins swirl into a treetop, like windblown leaves. Gaze skyward at a hawk circling slowly, the only sign of life on a hot afternoon. Peer through rose thorns at a nestful of blue green catbird's eggs. Watch robins mine a rain-soaked lawn for worms, cedar waxwings splash in the birdbath, a flicker flashing red brushstrokes as it wings into the forest.

Glimpses such as these are what make a backyard bird-watcher's heart beat faster—and turn casual observers into avian enthusiasts. Birds put on a show that's unsurpassed for sweet operatics and aerial ballet. It's free, open-air, and convenient; you can observe birds fluttering or perched virtually everywhere, from crowded cities to wild forests, from suburbia to seacoasts. At least some species stay nearby at all times of year, even during snowy winters when the rest of nature lies dormant.

To practiced observers, bird behavior can pinpoint the time of year and even foretell a change in the weather. Bird banding has shown that individuals of certain migrant species may stop off at the same garden where they enjoyed a good meal the previous year—arriving close to the same day and month. And folk wisdom credits birds with predicting storms (if they flock together at a feeder) or rainfall (the faster they fly, supposedly, the sooner it will rain).

A barometer these days of more than atmospheric changes, birds also alert ornithologists to ecological disturbances. In recent years, the National Academy of Science has reported a dramatic drop in the population of songbirds whose winter habitat—the rain forests of Central and South America—has been increasingly destroyed.

Ornithologists are not alone in their concern about the destiny and daily life of birds. According to the United States Department of the Interior, approximately a third of the U.S. population feeds or watches birds at least occasionally. If you're among them—or about to join their ranks—you can be classified as a bird-watcher or a birder.

A relatively casual interest is what usually distinguishes bird-watchers from birders, as the two terms are commonly used. A bird-watcher may join a local chapter of the Audubon Society to take field trips, attend programs, or participate in a Christmas count (see page 95)—a great way to get started. On the other hand, many bird-watchers travel no farther than their own backyard feeders and birdbaths.

A somewhat more zealous breed, birders are also known as field ornithologists. Their detailed knowledge of birds can be quite amazing, down to an ability to whistle bird songs or to identify which wild plants are favored by which species. Birders often focus on special interests: studying nest-building, habitats, or migration patterns, for instance, or photographing birds or using an artist's palette to capture the precise coloration of an olive-sided flycatcher. Some birders devote themselves to conservation efforts, and some travel all over the globe to add birds to their "life lists"—records of all the species they've ever identified.

Birder or bird-watcher, anyone who appreciates birds to any degree inevitably becomes a conservationist, too. It goes with the territory. One of the satisfactions of backyard bird-watching is that, by cultivating a habitat to attract birds, you can contribute in a small but valuable way to reclaiming the natural world for wildlife. To start, this may mean nothing more than allowing a few brambles to grow in a garden corner. But when many such birdscaped areas combine, the resulting patchwork can begin to offset some of the habitat losses caused by the rigors of civilization. At the same time, the garden bird-watcher gains chances to discover the joy of birds—reason enough.

This book is designed to serve as a primer for anyone who wants to attract birds to a garden or yard in North America. Even if you don't have a garden, this book can introduce you to the pleasures of bird-watching away from home. Its opening chapter, "Discovering Birds," explores such myster-ies as why warblers winter in the south and how to identify them when a dozen or so stop overnight in the crowns of your trees.

Chapter 2, "A Garden Guest List," can be left open near a window for quick reference as a field guide to garden birds. You'll find descriptions of 80 birds common to North American gardens and yards, along with an identifying photograph and range map for each species.

Plenty of wild bird food, shelter, and water are basic elements of hospitality that will draw birds to your property. In "Birdscaping Your Yard," Chapter 3, you'll find landscaping ideas and plant choices for creating a habitat with bird appeal—including such details as how to set up a reasonably catproof birdbath and how to grow a hummingbird's cafeteria of blooms.

For all you need to know about feeding seed, suet, and other favorite foods to birds, turn to Chapter 4, "A Wild Banquet." Supplementing nature's food will be especially comforting to your feathered friends if you live where winters are long, cold, and spare of vegetation.

If you want to add to the avian ambiance by constructing a rustic birdhouse or burbling garden pool, our last chapter, "Feeders, Houses & Baths," shows how with step-by-step directions and plans for 16 do-it-yourself projects.

Finally, we leave you with a resource list for learning more about birds on your own, as well as a checklist to help you record observations of your avian visitors. And now, outside the window, a yellow-bellied sapsucker hammers for attention . . . .

*Cedar waxwings devour
dogwood berries, and tree sparrow
perches on Pennisetum.*

*A canopy of autumn leaves
protectively reflects the vibrant
colors of an evening grosbeak (see
page 61). The bird's bill has evolved
for cracking large seeds.*

Discovering Birds

Birds have benefited people from earliest times. Inspiring artists, poets, and musicians with beauty and song, birds have also contributed their extraordinary example of flight as impetus to mankind's own quest to become airborne.

But for many people, the most appealing thing about birds is simply watching them. More than any other form of wildlife, birds provide a companionship as commonplace as clouds in the sky. They share our daily lives—soaring above the highway, roosting on a roof, warbling in a treetop, or splashing in a birdbath. Whether they show up singly, in pairs, or in flocks, birds help us to feel more alive, free, and in tune with nature.

This first chapter is designed to help you become better acquainted with birds and their ways—you'll learn what kinds of birds are most likely to visit residential neighborhoods, and how to identify them. The more you learn about your avian visitors—from their varied plumage to their elaborate nesting rituals—the more you'll enjoy your backyard bird-watching.

A Diverse Family Tree

More widespread than humans, birds inhabit virtually every niche of the globe capable of supporting life at all. Approximately 8,600 bird species live in areas from the Arctic to the Antarctic, from rain forests to deserts, from mountains to open seas. Birds have evolved into organisms as marvelously varied as the geographical areas they frequent.

Classifying birds

In biological classification, or taxonomy, all birds are grouped in the class *Aves*. This category encompasses about 170 bird families around the world, 78 of them represented in North America. Within these 78 families, more than 800 species have been observed north of Mexico. About a fifth of these originated in Europe, Asia, the Caribbean, or Mexico and are considered vagrants; the rest are indigenous to North America.

Traditional classification involves a hierarchy of groupings, each with a Latin name. The broadest subclassification of the class *Aves* is *order*, followed by *family;* an order may include one or many families of genetically related birds. *Genus* is a more specialized grouping, and the generic name always appears, capitalized, as the first word in a bird's scientific name. *Species* is a descriptive term that follows, narrowing the classification further. Some classifications involve subfamilies and subspecies, too. Here is how the black-headed grosbeak is classified:

- Order—*Passeriformes,* meaning "perching bird." This order includes 73 families of birds.

- Family—*Emberizidae,* meaning "members of the finch family."

- Subfamily—*Cardinalinae,* meaning "important" and "wearing red."

- Genus—*Pheucticus,* meaning "painted with cosmetics."

- Species—*melanocephalus,* meaning "black-headed."

The sequence of classification also reflects relative level of evolution, as well as relationships between birds. Loons, grebes, and pelicans, for example, as some of North America's most primitive birds, appear first in most field guides. The most highly evolved birds are members of the order *Passeriformes;* you'll find them listed last.

DNA and protein analysis, in recent years, has given ornithologists a more finely tuned approach to bird classification. As a result, the entire field of bird classification is in flux. Greater understanding of relationships between birds may lead to the division of some currently recognized species into two or more new ones, and some existing species may be grouped together as single species.

Backyard bird families

Bird families most likely to appear in a North American residential garden include hawks, game birds, pigeons, hummingbirds, woodpeckers, flycatchers, swallows, jays, chickadees, nuthatches, wrens, thrushes, vireos, warblers, grosbeaks, sparrows, blackbirds, orioles, tanagers, and finches.

Many birds will be attracted by particular plants or feeders; others will come to feed on the insects or even on the smaller birds in your garden. Here is a quick guide to some of them, listed in the order used in field guides. For more specific descriptions, see "A Garden Guest List," pages 20–61.

Game birds (family Phasianidae) feed at ground level. Note the chickenlike bills, feet, wings, and bodies of family members, which include grouse, quail, and pheasant. When surprised, game birds erupt from the ground and fly to nearby cover.

Pigeons and doves (family Columbidae), vegetarian ground-feeders, have heavy, rounded bodies, small heads, and thin bills.

Hummingbirds (family Trochilidae), tiny and colorful, have thin bills that evolved for sucking nectar from flowers. Most are migratory. (See page 79.)

Woodpeckers (family Picidae) depend on trees as a source of insects. In spring, listen for rhythmic drumming. Flickers typically feed at ground level on ants. Family traits include a sturdy bill, a stiff tail, and toes designed for clinging vertically to branches or trunks.

Flycatchers (family Tyrannidae) snatch insects in the air, darting from a perch and then returning to the same branch or one nearby. Some have surprisingly heavy bills for insectivores. These birds are mostly migratory, and few species are present in winter.

Jays, crows, and magpies (family Corvidae) are all cousins, but various species of jay are the family members most often seen in gardens across North America. Mid-sized, raucous birds, they'll eat almost anything and tend to dominate garden feeders.

Titmice and chickadees (family Paridae) are small, grayish insectivores that may be seen feeding in trees—or, in winter, at a suet feeder.

Nuthatches (family Sittidae) hop down tree trunks while feeding on insects. Small, gray-backed, and dark-capped, they share many of the woodpecker's feeding habits.

Wrens (family Troglodytidae) sing varied, often beautiful songs. Small, chunky, and brown, with stubby, upturned tails, these insectivores favor shrubs and low ground cover.

Thrushes, kinglets, and bluebirds (family Muscicapidae) are erect-standing birds that vary from small to robin-size. They eat insects and fruit.

Vireos (family Vireonidae), green or gray, are small and relatively slow-flying. These highly migratory insectivores usually visit only wooded gardens that can supply their dietary or nesting needs.

Warblers, grosbeaks, buntings, sparrows, blackbirds, orioles, and tanagers (family Emberizidae) are genetically related within a huge family of diverse subgroups. Small, colorful, and extremely active insectivores, warblers flock in large mixes (perhaps six or more species) during spring and fall migrations, when they may pass through wooded gardens. Grosbeaks, sparrows, and buntings (including cardinals) are small to mid-sized, with heavy bills for cracking seeds. Vividly colored blackbirds, orioles, and tanagers, larger than other family members, are attracted to seed feeders, especially in winter.

Finches (family Fringillidae), small to medium-sized seed-eaters with heavy bills, are usually brown, yellow, or red.

Notice the family resemblance shared by five different birds in the shape of wings, tails, and sharply pointed bills.

Brown-headed Cowbird

Bobolink

Western Meadowlark

Red-winged Blackbird

Northern Oriole

Anatomy Through Evolution

American kestrel has strong, hooked bill for tearing flesh and crushing bones of small animal prey.

Hairy woodpecker's straight, sturdy bill functions as chisel to hammer into tree and capture insects.

Ruby-throated hummingbird uses long, slender bill to feed on nectar and insects deep inside tubular flowers.

Red-eyed vireo's slender bill is adapted for capturing, holding, and crushing insects.

Song sparrow has heavy, triangular bill for grasping and crushing seeds.

Over millions of years of evolution, birds have adapted to diverse conditions all over the globe. For the ostrich and other large, flightless birds of flat regions, running on strong legs was the most significant survival skill. At the opposite extreme, the tiny songbird's evolution gave it three forward-pointing toes and one pointing backward, enabling it to perch safely to rest after astonishingly long flights.

While the ostrich represents a primitive level of bird evolution, the songbird is considered by ornithologists to be the most anatomically advanced.

Descendants of dinosaurs

The earliest "birds" resembled feathered dinosaurs. Dating from approximately 150 million years ago, fossils of the *archyaeopteryx* (meaning "ancient wing") reveal creatures with clawed wings, toothed bills, bony tails, and heavy bones. It seems unlikely that they did much flying; probably they hopped on the ground or glided from tree to tree.

Birds more closely resembling modern forms—such as loons and pelicans—did not appear until 60 million years ago, as shown by fossil records. By one million years ago, all of today's bird families had come into existence.

Specialized anatomies

All birds today share certain anatomical characteristics. All are warm-blooded, feathered creatures with wings (though not all can fly). All have hornlike bills and scaled legs and feet. Their lightweight, hollow bones make it easier to stay airborne, and a clavicle—or wishbone—anchors their massive breast muscles for flight.

Surviving for so long in the earth's great environmental diversity, however, birds have also had to evolve many specialized anatomical characteristics. Variations in body parts and color help birds exist in widely differing landscapes.

Bills of every size and shape have evolved through the ages, to assure successful feeding in diverse habitats. Most ducks, for example, have broad, spatulate bills that can sift aquatic plant and animal food from muddy water. Pelicans have enough room for a hearty portion of fish in their bills.

Woodpeckers have specialized bills, bones, and muscles that absorb the impact of hammering into trees for wood-boring insects. They've also evolved an extremely long tongue for capturing insects deep inside drilled holes or crevices.

Bird-watching in your garden, you may also notice the broad bills of seedeaters such as grosbeaks, finches, and sparrows, designed to crack seed hulls. By contrast, vireos, wrens, warblers, and flycatchers have thinner bills for snatching insects.

Feet and wings are specialized, too. While a duck's webbed feet are adapted for swimming, a woodpecker's large feet and broad tail keep the bird stable while clinging to trees as it drills for food. Ground-feeding birds, such as the brown thrasher, often have feet proportionately larger than those of chickadees or warblers, which glean insects from leafy vegetation.

The long, pointed wings of American kestrels, swifts, and swallows have evolved for lengthy flying. The comparatively short wings of wrens, on the other hand, are adapted for quick shuttles from one clump of brush or shrubbery to another. An owl's specialized feather structure allows it to fly silently through the night in search of small prey, such as deer mice, that have keen hearing.

Birds have evolved a variety of flight techniques, too. Small songbirds flap their wings in energetic up-and-down strokes. Tiny hummingbirds hover as they beat their wings 70 times a second. Hawks soar gracefully on air currents, and most species glide at least occasionally—more slowly and over more distance in the case of bigger birds.

The penguin uses its wings as flippers after diving into icy arctic water; the swimming motion is the same as the flying movements of other birds. Though this large bird does not fly today, it's believed that it once did.

Adaptive colors are often the first specialization we notice in birds. In some species, males and females appear identical in color; in others, the male is bright and the female relatively dull.

Coloration can serve more than one survival need. The male finch's vivid plumage is used for courting females as well as for territorial defense. It is also believed to be a means of communicating with other finches. The red-winged blackbird displays its red epaulettes both to attract a female and to ward off males competing for its nesting territory. Ground-feeding birds are protected by feathers that seem to blend into the surrounding landscape.

Owl's talons can capture and kill prey as well as hold it while it is being eaten.

Woodpeckers can cling to vertical branches, using two forward and two backward toes and sharp claws.

Quail's stout forward toes are needed to scratch the ground for food.

Sparrows have three forward toes and a backward one for grasping branches, allowing feeding and roosting in trees and shrubs.

Bird Behavior

Whether fluffing feathers against the cold or flapping wings in graceful flight, birds are a joy to watch. Birds make a garden seem more vibrantly alive. A tiny Wilson's warbler flies into view, flits about snatching insects, then disappears in an instant into a neighbor's yard. A fox sparrow darts from shrubby cover near the lawn, scratches the grass for hidden seeds, then flutters back to its hiding place, only to repeat the same movements over and over for half an hour.

Observing bird behavior will help you identify just which species have come to visit, feed, bathe, and perhaps build a nest on your property. Keeping a record of the specific behaviors adds greatly to the pleasure of bird-watching.

Besides distinguishing a brown creeper from a winter wren, bird behavior marks the changing seasons. Once familiar with it, you can stay alert for migratory visitors or changing plumage.

Breeding rituals

From courtship displays to intricate nest making, birds' breeding behavior in spring has been specialized through evolution to ensure each species' reproductive success.

Claiming territory, courting a mate, building a nest, and hatching eggs fill the busy springtime agenda for many birds, such as this yellow warbler.

Claiming and defending a territory is the first challenge for many male birds. This territory, which may include your entire garden or a portion of it, needs to provide food, water, and a secure nest site. Attracting a mate with song and display is the next order of business. Finally, the bird faces the task of protecting its territory, mate, and young from intruders.

Hummingbirds perform elaborate, sweeping courtship displays on the wing; these may take the form of great aerial J, U, or O formations. Though quite different, the rhythmic drumming and exaggerated posturing of the downy woodpecker serve the same purpose. For most birds, these breeding rituals take place in the spring. But some birds, like the mockingbird, hold and defend feeding territories year-round, which explains their aggressive behavior and unseasonal singing.

As spring continues, you may see birds carrying nesting materials—perhaps a bit of grass or yarn, or some small twigs or even sticks. Each bird has its own distinctive style of construction, from the robin's cuplike mud and grass home to the bushtit's nest resembling a delicate sock of spider web, lichen, and grass. Thus, the nest itself is a good clue to the bird's identity.

Survival skills

After breeding, the focus of bird behavior shifts to simply staying alive. First and foremost is the search for food. Many birds have developed specialized skills to meet this task. The towhee scrapes the ground with both feet to unearth insects. The kingfisher dives head first for fish. The nuthatch travels head first down a tree trunk as it forages for tiny bugs. And for many species, extraordinary feats of migratory flight are necessary to find enough food for survival (see page 14).

Between meals—and flights—all birds occasionally bathe, preen, or dust themselves. Fluffing feathers, huddling in a row, and tucking their heads under their wings are ways for birds to stay warm in freezing weather or at night.

Other intriguing kinds of behavior defend birds against predators. Head bobbing is thought to help birds keep a sharp lookout from many angles. "Mobbing" is a group effort by numerous birds to harass a predator, such as a hawk, until it leaves (see facing page).

Twitters, Trills & Chirps

Just as fragrant flowers in a garden delight our sense of smell, so do melodious birds bring pleasure to our ears. Symbol of springtime and inspiration for poets and composers, bird song is also an identification tag for the various species.

Actually, birds chirp (or "call") at least as much as they sing series of notes. More than a free outdoor concert, singing and calling are their basic ways of communicating.

As the breeding season gets under way in spring, males sing to attract females—and to discourage intruders (usually males of the same species) from encroaching on their territory.

Males, and sometimes females, are apt to keep singing throughout the nesting cycle. In warmer areas, this may begin as early as February and continue until July. Songs diminish as fledglings leave the nest. Though some species, like the mockingbird, sing in certain regions throughout the year, even they are more vocal during the breeding season.

Song is certainly the most beautiful of bird sounds, but the brief, sharp calls made throughout the year hold considerable interest for birders. These chirps and squeaks are believed to serve less aggressive purposes than songs—perhaps warning of a predator or announcing to other birds that food is available. The nasal chatter of red-breasted nuthatches as they flutter through a wooded lot keeps the flock together during its constant foraging.

These feeding and gathering calls—for many small birds— are most likely to be heard in the morning and late afternoon. But at any time of day you may hear the excited calls of a mixed flock of woodpeckers, jays, chickadees, nuthatches, warblers, and finches joining together to mob a resting Cooper's hawk or screech owl. The raucous clatter will continue until the harassed predator flies well beyond the flock's feeding range and leaves the mob members in peace.

In many cities, the range of bird sounds you are likely to hear has been expanded by birds released from captivity, both deliberately and accidentally. Populations of canary-winged parakeets, rose-ringed parakeets, and monk parrots add their various shrieks, screeches, and squawks to the banter of more melodious urban bird residents.

Some bird sounds are consistent throughout an entire species; in others, such as the white-crowned sparrow, there can be so much variation that the trained ear can detect two distinct local dialects within one small city. Some birds—the phoebe and the chickadee, for instance— have been named for the distinctive sounds they make. Others, like the European nightingale or the American black-headed and rose-breasted grosbeaks, are renowned for the melody of their song. The mourning dove is distinguished by its low, mournful sound, something like the owl's.

Mimicking other birds is a specialty of jays, mockingbirds, and starlings; on rare occasions, even warblers and finches imitate other species. Just why they do this is unknown, but mimicry probably enhances a basic song, making it more attractive to females.

Birders use song to help identify birds, and tape recordings of bird songs and calls are available through birders' mail order catalogs and periodicals. Or you might consider making your own tapes. A good cassette recorder and directional microphone are all you need to make your own recordings to capture the avian operatics in your garden.

By mimicking, you can sometimes attract a few curious birds. Make a "pishing" sound by enunciating *p*, followed by *sh*. Repeat it softly in a series: *pshhh-pshhh-pshhh*. If a chickadee is perched nearby, it may come out to investigate. Be sure not to disrupt nesting or territorial birds this way or with taped songs.

Songs and calls of individual species are described in "A Garden Guest List," pages 20–61.

Migratory Marathons

In one of the most amazing seasonal phenomena that a backyard birder can witness, vast migrations of birds cross North America each spring and fall. Only a few migrants are likely to be attracted to a garden, but you'll learn to recognize certain species coming to spend the summer or others that winter with you.

If you keep records over a period of years, you'll see that a number of migrant birds do use your yard for a day, or perhaps a week, during spring or fall. With time and attention, you'll be able to predict their arrival and departure within a week or two.

Amazing feats

Some birds' flights defy belief. The arctic tern, for example, traverses as many as 22,000 miles in its annual migration. From breeding grounds in arctic and subarctic North America, Asia, and Europe, it flies as far south as coastal Antarctica.

Many common backyard birds undertake marathon migrations, too. The barn swallow flies from North American gardens to wintering grounds in Brazil and Argentina. Delicate though they might seem, many hummingbirds also head south for the winter, flying to Mexico, Central America, and South America. The tiny ruby-throated hummingbird is known to fly nonstop across the Gulf of Mexico.

How high? When they're not migrating, most birds fly no higher than 50 to 100 feet above the tops of trees. In migration they fly higher, but most species seldom exceed 1,000 feet above ground. However, records do exist for birds seen at 20,000 to 25,000 feet high, a few even higher. Waterfowl, hawks, vultures, swifts, and swallows seem to be among North America's highest-flying birds. But even these fly at their top altitudes as the exception, not the rule.

How fast? Most birds fly between 20 and 50 miles per hour, but in an emergency they can exceed these speeds. The dunlin, a shorebird, has been clocked in excess of 100 miles per hour. Peregrine falcons have been recorded at 175 miles per hour.

Though most birds are much slower, they can still cover amazing distances in short periods of time. The nocturnally migrating blackpoll warbler travels from 30 to 200 or more miles in one night, depending on weather conditions.

Flight paths

Birds migrate through aerial corridors called flyways. Following coastlines, river systems, or mountain ranges, the primary routes in North America are known as the Pacific, Central, Mississippi, and Atlantic flyways.

There are various theories explaining how flocks of migrating birds find their way across such long distances: it appears that different species use different environmental clues to guide them to distant breeding or wintering grounds. Night-fliers may orient themselves by the stars or the earth's magnetic field. Birds that fly by day may use the sun, the magnetic field, or such landmarks as rivers, mountain ranges, or seacoasts.

But birds fly not only from north to south and back, but also between east and west and mountains and plains. They follow the course of a season's flower crop or the abundance of insect hatches. Furthermore, bird banding shows that individual birds may return to the same backyard year after year throughout their life spans. Birds sometimes migrate to areas far beyond the major flyways. No matter where you live in North America, migratory birds may drop by your garden occasionally.

Looking for greener pastures

Birds fly south for the winter, it was long believed, to avoid cold, snowy weather. Most migrate for food as it becomes unavailable in winter. Also, recent research tells us that many of our migrant backyard birds are actually tropical species that simply go back home in winter. During their spring and summer breeding season, they're drawn to North America by the abundance and variety of food and nesting sites to be found here.

As the face of our landscape has changed, so have migratory patterns. Whereas bird habitats might once have been isolated grasslands, forests, or deserts, the world has been vastly altered by farming, highway construction, and urbanization. Some habitats have been destroyed, at the expense of many species, and others created or opened up. Mockingbirds traveled northward with urbanization, which provided rooftops and low gardens similar to their original West Coast habitat on desert margins. Brewer's blackbirds and house finches expanded their ranges eastward as farms turned formerly inhospitable land into rich habitats.

The presence of cities across North America has also warmed certain local climates just enough to allow small numbers of migratory species to cling to life in winter where they otherwise could not.

Disappearing rain forests

The destruction of tropical rain forests in Central and South America, and elsewhere, has had a disastrous effect on birds. As rain forest habitats disappear, many of the birds supported by them—some of which migrate to North America—are threatened with extinction.

We already know that the migratory songbird population is declining. Normal population fluctuations, yearly shifts in areas used by various species, and the vastness of most migrants' ranges make it difficult for ornithologists to exactly assess the scope of this decline. Still, the clearing of tropical rain forests is expected to continue to reduce—or eliminate—certain species that presently visit our yards. Last year's warbler flock of seven species, for ex-

ample, may include only three next year. Wood thrushes that now nest in the garden may vanish, to be replaced by a species that does not depend on a tropical habitat for survival during six to eight months of the year.

Staying through winter

Gradually increasing numbers of migratory birds now remain far north of their 19th-century winter ranges as their needs are met by special plantings and supplemental feedings in gardens across the continent. No species has abandoned migration entirely, but individual birds have learned to use certain garden plants, bird feeders, and baths to survive through the winter.

Northern orioles were among the pioneers of this new pattern. Many thrushes, warblers, sparrows, blackbirds, and finches have also taken advantage of northern gardens. As more people provide supplemental food, water, and good habitat conditions, the trend seems likely to increase.

Snow geese storm the pewter sky over Klamath Basin on the California-Oregon border, a national wildlife refuge where millions of migrating waterfowl stop each year.

Identifying Birds

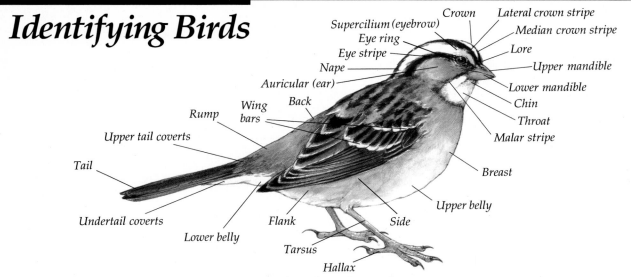

Anatomy of a White-throated Sparrow

Learning to identify birds precisely and accurately is basic to birding, at home or afield. Along with the experience you accumulate, the basic tools of identification are binoculars (see facing page), a good field guide (see page 109), and a notebook for recording what you observe.

Looking for clues

Birders identify species by exact characteristics, such as wing markings, and also relative ones, such as size. As shown in the drawing above, a bird's tiny body, when magnified through binoculars, displays numerous clues to its identity.

Colors—on the back, underside, tail, head, breast, and elsewhere—are often the first field marks you will notice. While the colors of some species (the painted bunting, for example) are vibrantly obvious, more subtle tones are characteristic of many birds, such as the eastern phoebe and the pine siskin. Even within a species, color may vary by sex, age, diet, season, and geographical location.

Size is usually measured in comparison with a familiar bird, such as a sparrow, robin, or crow. Just note whether what you see is about the same size, smaller, or larger.

Shape of the bill, head, legs, wings, and tail helps you distinguish between species. The downy and hairy woodpeckers look quite similar, but the hairy's bill is heavy and about the length of its head, while the downy's is only about half that size and thinner.

Markings are often noteworthy, such as wing bars, eye rings, any pattern on the head or neck, or streaking on the back or breast.

Field guide & notebook

A field guide illustrates and describes birds in a particular geographic area, such as the western United States or North America. Most field guides are organized in taxonomic categories. The second half contains information about backyard birds.

Study and check off birds in your guide or on page 110 of this book as you identify them in your garden. If you think you're seeing mostly sparrows and finches, for example, mark those that the guide's text or range maps show in your locality; paperclip the pages for quick reference later. When you see a familiar bird, such as a robin, look it up to learn more about it and other birds that could be mistaken for it. Also read to learn the migratory patterns of birds that appear only briefly and seasonally.

Keeping a record of birds that visit your property can add richly to the satisfaction you get from your garden. A birding notebook usually starts as a simple list of birds seen during a day. If you can't identify a bird but can narrow down the possibilities to two or three similar species, note their names and any comments that may help you with a more precise identification the next time you see the bird.

Include the date of each observation, as well as the time of day and the weather conditions. Within a few years, the notebook will start to reflect both seasonal changes and population fluctuations.

Choosing Binoculars

Since birding is visual—and since birds are small and quick to fly away—it's obvious why binoculars are important to anyone interested in sighting the first American tree sparrow of winter or the first pine warbler of spring. Choosing a pair is easy if you know what to look for.

Binoculars are commonly sold by a numerical description, such as 7 x 35. The first number tells how many times the binoculars magnify the image; the second gives the diameter in millimeters of the objective lenses (farthest from the eyes). The bigger these lenses, the more light they gather and the better you can see in shadow, at dawn, or at dusk.

For birding, get something in the 7x to 10x magnification range (go to the higher power if you can hold the binoculars steady, a skill that will improve amazingly with practice). If you expect to bird-watch at twilight or after dark, buy a pair with large objective lenses. As a rule of thumb, divide the binoculars' second number by the first one (for example, 35 divided by 7). If the dividend is 5 or greater, the binoculars will provide adequate light for birding. You'll also find that wide field, or wide angle, lenses work best for finding and following fast-moving birds.

Focus systems on binoculars vary. For birding, choose a fast-focus system with center focusing wheel that goes from infinity to near focus in one revolution or so. Extra-close focus is a real advantage for spotting perching birds. Smooth and even focusing is an important feature to test for when shopping. On waterproof binoculars, focusing may be stiff at first, but it will ease up with use.

Binoculars are made with either a roof prism or a porro prism. The roof-prism type has a straight barrel and is therefore more compact. It's also about 15% lighter in weight—but more expensive. The porro-prism type, which has the classic center dog-leg, is bulkier but generally costs less. On either type, look for multicoated lenses, which improve light transmission noticeably.

Choose binoculars that give a clear, crisp, single image without warps or blurring. Look through the lenses toward a light source and check for a prism effect around the image edge—don't buy any that give such a distortion.

If you wear glasses, you can buy a pair of binoculars with roll-down or retractable rubber eye cups which at least partially improve viewing.

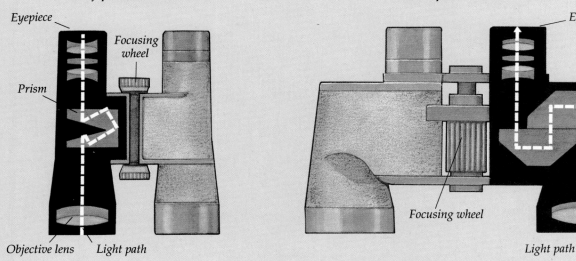

Roof-prism binoculars

Eyepiece

Focusing wheel

Prism

Objective lens   Light path

Porro-prism binoculars

Eyepiece

Prism

Focusing wheel

Light path   Objective lens

Home, Sweet Habitat

Food, water, protective cover, and a safe place to raise young are the essentials of life that a habitat provides for birds as well as for all other living creatures.

Birds have adapted themselves to habitats nearly as diverse as the globe itself, from arctic tundra to tropical rain forests and from cityscapes to open prairies. Even the birds that visit our backyards—only a fraction of the world bird population—are accustomed to a variety of habitats.

The male northern cardinal brings bright red color to suburban gardens on the East Coast, where plantings re-create its wild habitat of shrubs, thickets, and woodland streams. The *sweet-sweet* that opens the long song of the yellow warbler might be heard near open deciduous woodlands and scrubby areas near water, while the Anna's hummingbird shows up abundantly along the Pacific slope in open areas varying from desert to chaparral to forest's edge.

The changing environment

Bird habitats are defined, in part, by environmental conditions and plant types. Open ocean, coastlines, salt or freshwater wetlands, rivers, and lakes together form aquatic habitats. Forests, grasslands, meadows, chaparrals, deserts, and tundras are terrestrial habitats.

During the past century and a half, the habitats of North American birds have changed radically. Civilization reshaped the land as it spread across the continent. Eastern forests were cut down, mountains leveled, prairies plowed, marshes and ponds drained, and arid regions made green by irrigation. Some birds responded by restricting themselves to their ever-shrinking original habitats; this has resulted in the extinction of some species, like the ivory-billed woodpecker, and in decreased population for most species.

Other species have adapted more resourcefully, increasing their ranges to cultivated fields, islands of trees, or the varied garden habitats provided by towns, suburbs, and even cities. The mockingbird, cardinal, and house finch are three of the many species that have widened their ranges in this way.

Amazingly, even high-rise "canyons" and highway "rivers" approximate certain habitat conditions for some species. The "cliff" faces of downtown business districts have long been home to the rock dove, a European species. More recently, the peregrine falcon has adapted to the city as a habitat niche.

Power poles and fences, dams and reservoirs, and urban growth have all had a plus-and-minus effect. But pollution—of air, water, and land—and

Along a rural roadside in the West, juicy wild blackberries ripen in late summer to the delight of robins, towhees, and a thrasher. Nearby, bushtits sample seeds of white yarrow, a goldfinch dines on a teasel, while in the distance a meadowlark spreads its wings and barn swallows swoop toward the barn.

the increasing loss of habitat to civilization have threatened bird life worldwide.

Living on the edge

Edges, also called "ecotones," are focal points of productivity for both birds and bird-watchers. In these borderline areas of mixed vegetation, two or more habitats come together—for example, a forest opens into a meadow, or a field joins the willows and cattails on a pond's bank. A gardener can imitate such edge conditions (see pages 64–83).

With the right mix of trees, shrubs, vines, ground cover, and lawn, the needs of many different species can be met. A flock of warblers may feed on insects from trees before flying south for winter. A month later, cedar waxwings and robins may descend on berries newly ripened on vines. As nuthatches glean insects from tree branches, finches find seeds on the ground, fleeing to cover in thorny shrubs when a cat prowls through the garden. Spring brings a hummingbird, scouting for places to build its all-but-invisible lichen and cobweb nest.

Trees, rock walls, hedgerows, and fence posts are typical places where birds find niches for nests. Barns, sheds, and even houses also provide nest sites, and sometimes insect and plant food as well.

(If a woodpecker decides to scavenge for supper by hammering on the walls of your garage, check for wood-boring insects.)

House sparrows seem to favor nesting under terra cotta roof tiles. Tar and gravel rooftops are sometimes used by killdeer for nesting. Chimney swifts and barn swallows like the perpendicular aspect of walls and chimneys. Small ledges are sometimes enough for a black phoebe or robin.

The comforts of home

When developing a habitat for birds at home, it's wise to have it fit the general natural ecology of your area. A cactus garden is unlikely to attract birds in a moist, nondesert climate. On the other hand, a grove of native conifers may be a prime stopover choice for weary migrants.

Watch and listen for birds in parks and gardens near your home, noting the trees, shrubs, vines, and ground covers where they prefer to congregate. Adding the ideas and specific suggestions on pages 64–83 in this book, you can arrive at a rich habitat plan for your own property. You may even wish to expand your plan by involving the whole neighborhood, a school, or a local park.

Grow mostly plants that are native to your area to be of greatest service to birds. If enough yards are planted for wildlife, they will begin to compensate for lost natural habitats.

A Garden Guest List

Birds bring unique delight to daily life and drama to each season. Watching these beautiful feathered guests in our yards—as they fly, eat, bathe, fight, court, build nests, and raise young—draws us closer to nature and may develop into a fascinating hobby.

In the next 40 pages, you'll find a brief description and an identifying photograph for each of 80 species of North American birds. For our "guest list," we selected those birds that most commonly appear in backyards and gardens across the continent. Each entry also includes a map showing the bird's typical range—in winter, the spring-summer breeding season, or all year. Each listing indicates how to attract the bird by either supplemental feed or plantings.

To get to know each bird even better—as well as to read about many more species than we have space to describe here—consult a good field guide for North America or for your specific region. Several are listed on page 109.

The order in which birds are presented in this chapter, as well as their English common names and Latin scientific names, is consistent with the most recent edition of the Check-List of North American Birds, prepared by the American Ornithologists' Union. This sequence places species in their presumed ancestral relationships from the "lowest" or most primitive to the "highest" or most recently evolved.

Lodged out of harm's way in a pine tree, a nest of mud and grass holds eggs which the female robin broods for about 2 weeks (see page 45).

American Kestrel (Sparrow Hawk) *Falco sparverius*

Winter
Breeding
All year

Identification: This robin-sized bird of prey with long, pointed wings is the smallest and most common falcon in North America. It has a reddish brown back and tail, overall black barring, and two vertical black stripes on each side of its white face; males are distinguished by slate blue wings and crown. Young American kestrels look like males but are more heavily barred.

Voice: When alarmed, kestrels will call a shrill, ringing *killy, killy, killy, killy.*

Behavior: Kestrels often sit on power lines or poles watching for prey, or hover over grassy fields. Once prey is sighted, the little falcon folds its wings and dives, grasping its victim in its talons and carrying it to a nearby perch to consume whole or in large pieces.

Habitat: Open grasslands. The adaptable kestrel is common in cities, in suburbs, and along highways.

Natural food: Insects, lizards, snakes, rodents (particularly mice), and an occasional songbird.

Nest: Natural tree cavities or woodpecker holes are preferred nesting sites, but kestrels may nest in birdhouses. Their 4 or 5 oval eggs are white or light cinnamon-colored, covered with small brown dots; they require 29 to 31 days of incubation, mostly by the female. The young leave the nest about a month after hatching.

How to attract: Kestrels may nest in a birdhouse (8 by 8 by 14 inches high with a 3-inch entrance hole) raised 10 to 30 feet above ground on a pole or tall tree in an open area.

Ring-necked Pheasant *Phasianus colchicus*

Winter
Breeding
All year

Identification: A native of Asia, the ring-necked pheasant was introduced successfully in North America more than 100 years ago and has done very well here. The 30- to 36-inch-long male is among the most spectacular of all birds, with its extravagant, multicolored, iridescent plumage, brilliant red face, green head, and long, tapering tail. The female is distinctly less showy, with buff plumage and a shorter tail.

Voice: When flushed, the male cackles in alarm. A courting male crows like a rooster, then whirrs its wings.

Behavior: A male pheasant defends a breeding territory of a couple of acres against other males in order to win the right to mate with the three or four hens living there. To escape danger, a pheasant will usually run rather than fly.

Habitat: Prairies, brushy fields, and cropland.

Natural food: Grains from fields, weed seeds, and berries from old fields; also insects in spring, such as grasshoppers, caterpillars, and beetles.

Nest: These birds build a grassy nest on the ground in a natural hollow surrounded by protective vegetation. Their 10 to 12 brownish buff eggs are incubated by the female for 23 to 25 days, and the chicks are able to leave the nest within a day.

How to attract: Pheasants may be attracted to seed offered at or near ground level. They like weedy garden edges near agricultural fields.

Northern Bobwhite *Colinus virginianus*

Identification: This plump little fowl is the classic "quail" of the East. A 10-inch, chickenlike bird with a short tail, the bobwhite is a mottled red brown in color. The male has a white throat and a white eye stripe; the female is all buff.

Voice: The species is named for the bright *bob, bob-white* whistle that the male often calls from a fence post in the spring. Its quiet *ka-loi-kee* call is uttered to assemble a family or covey.

Behavior: After the breeding season, several families join together to form coveys that forage by day and sleep together at night in a tight circle, tails toward the center. When threatened, the covey flushes, each bird flying out of the circle in the direction it is facing.

Habitat: Farmland, open meadows, weedy pastures, and open woodland.

Natural food: Cropland grain and weed seeds most of the year, but also green shoots, insects, and berries in spring and summer.

Nest: A pair of bobwhites will build their nest on the ground in a depression under an arch of dead grasses. Their 14 to 16 creamy white eggs are incubated by both parents for 23 or 24 days. The chicks follow their parents away from the nest within a day of hatching. Bobwhites produce at least 2 broods a year.

How to attract: Bobwhites appear regularly in backyards and gardens where a birdseed mixture is spread on the ground. Weedy areas near thick cover may also attract them.

Winter
Breeding
All year

Gambel's Quail *Callipepla gambelii*

Identification: Short and rotund, the chickenlike gray Gambel's quail is distinguished by a teardrop-shaped plume on the forecrown. The 11-inch fowl has chestnut sides streaked with white; the male has a black face and throat, a chestnut cap, and a black patch in the middle of his buff belly, while the female is gray and brown.

Voice: Calls of the Gambel's quail vary from a loud *chi-ca-go-go* to grunts and chuckles used to locate the flock.

Behavior: Like other quail species, the Gambel's lives in coveys that may total 40 or more birds outside the breeding season. The covey usually roosts in low shrubs at night, often near a water hole or creek that it can visit in early morning and late afternoon.

Habitat: Dry or desert bottomland where scrub and sagebrush grow.

Natural food: Primarily seeds, leaves, shoots, and buds of green desert plants; also some insects and fruit.

Nest: The Gambel's pair builds its nest of dry grasses on or near the ground under desert shrubs. The 10 to 12 dull white to pale buff eggs, marked with brown, are incubated by the female for 21 to 24 days. The chicks are almost immediately led from the nest, single file, by the male, with the female bringing up the rear.

How to attract: These desert birds frequent backyards and gardens offering water holes or birdbaths at ground level near abundant cover. They like birdseed, as long as cover is close by.

Winter
Breeding
All year

Killdeer *Charadrius vociferus*

Winter
Breeding
All year

Identification: The best-known member of the plover family, the killdeer is a 10-inch bird with a brown back and white belly interrupted by two distinct black bands (across the upper breast and neck), a white collar, and a white spot above red-rimmed eyes. In flight, its reddish rump and white wing bars show. Male and female look alike.

Voice: The killdeer is named for its familiar *kill-dee, kill-dee, kill-dee* call heard across open landscapes most of the year.

Behavior: To protect its nest or young from predators, an adult killdeer will convincingly feign a broken wing while calling a loud *trrrrrrrrrr* to lure intruders away. On the ground, the birds typically run short distances, then stand still, then run again.

Habitat: Often far from water and close to human habitation—roadsides, driveways, airports, cemeteries, parking lots, and cultivated fields.

Natural food: Mostly insects (about 98 percent of its diet), such as grasshoppers, beetles, ants, caterpillars, grubs, and spiders; also weed seeds gleaned from old fields.

Nest: The killdeer builds no nest. It simply lays its 4 blotched brown oval eggs in a depression on open ground, usually surrounded by gravel or assorted debris. Incubation is by both adults for 24 to 26 days; the chicks leave the nest as soon as they are dry. Two broods a year are common.

How to attract: Beaches and spacious gravel areas near water may attract killdeer as nesting sites.

Rock Dove (Pigeon) *Columba livia*

Winter
Breeding
All year

Identification: Better known as a barn or city "pigeon," the 14-inch rock dove is found in a variety of color forms developed through domestication. Yet most rock doves resemble their wild ancestors—gray overall with darker heads, iridescent purple necks, and white rumps. Male and female look alike.

Voice: A rock dove's call is a soft *coo-a-roo, coo-ru-coooo, coo-a-coo.* A courting male will utter similar coos while dancing before his mate.

Behavior: The name "rock dove" comes from the attraction of the wild birds to rocks, cliffs, and ledges in their native Europe and Asia. They have adapted well in cities to the ledges of buildings, bridges, and monuments, and in the countryside to the lofts and beams of barns.

Habitat: Buildings and other man-made structures in North American cities and suburbs.

Natural food: Grains and green sprouts on farms, bread crumbs and garbage in cities.

Nest: Shallow and flimsy platform nests of grasses, straw, and other debris are built by rock doves atop ledges and building beams and under bridges. Both adults share the incubation of their 2 white eggs for 17 to 19 days. The young are in the nest for more than a month before they can fly. Several broods a year are typical.

How to attract: "Pigeons" are often unwanted but eager seed eaters at urban feeding stations and water areas. They're messy, and they intimidate smaller birds.

Mourning Dove   *Zenaida macroura*

Identification: A classic wild dove, the mourning dove is a slender 12-inch bird (including its long, pointed tail) that is overall gray brown with scattered black spots and a pinkish wash on its breast. Male and female look alike. In flight, the tail shows white edges and the wings produce a whistle.

Voice: Its melancholy *cwoo-ah, cwoo, cwoo, cwoo* call gives the mourning dove its common name. By counting males' coos in the spring, biologists can take a census of breeding pairs.

Behavior: This bird could have been called a "morning" dove—it is most active between the hours of 7 and 9 A.M. The young are fed "pigeon milk," a granular fluid produced in the adult crop and pumped directly into the nestlings' mouths by both male and female.

Habitat: Suburban gardens, farms, and parks throughout North America, especially near water.

Natural food: Almost entirely grain and seeds of weeds and grasses, eaten at ground level.

Nest: A flimsy nest of sticks built in a tree supports 2 white eggs, incubated by both parents for 13 or 14 days. The young leave the nest 2 weeks after hatching. A mourning dove pair may produce 2 to 5 broods each summer.

How to attract: Mourning doves are easily attracted by offering cracked corn and smaller grains in tray feeders on or near the ground. Water also entices them, as do coniferous trees where they may nest.

Winter
Breeding
All year

Screech Owl (Eastern & Western)   *Otus asio, Otus kennicottii*

Identification: At 9 inches, the screech owl is one of the smallest owls with ear tufts in North America. The eastern screech owl may be either red or gray; the western screech owl (pictured at right) is usually gray with a darker bill. Both sexes look alike.

Voice: Despite their name, screech owls do not screech. The eastern emits a tremulous, eerie cry in the night. The western gives a rhythmic series of whistles.

Behavior: In winter, screech owls roost during daylight in tree cavities or birdhouses and can often be seen at dusk sitting in the entrance holes, half asleep.

Habitat: Forests, farm woodlots, and shade trees in urban and suburban backyards and parks.

Natural food: Mice, shrews, large insects, small reptiles, amphibians, songbirds, small game birds, and small birds of prey—including other screech owls. Hunting begins soon after dark.

Nest: These cavity nesters will appropriate woodpecker holes and large birdhouses as places in which to lay their 4 or 5 pure white eggs. The female incubates the eggs while the male brings food to her during the 21 to 30 days required for the eggs to hatch. Youngsters leave the nest a month later.

How to attract: Screech owls will roost and/or nest in large birdhouses (8 by 8 by 14 inches high with a 3-inch entrance hole) located 10 to 30 feet above the ground in mature trees, such as large oaks. Dead trees provide nest sites, too. Screech owls will drink and bathe in garden ponds at night.

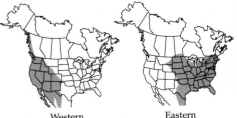

Western   Eastern

Great Horned Owl *Bubo virginianus*

Winter
Breeding
All year

Identification: A large owl with ear tufts, the 22-inch great horned owl is a striking bird with mottled brown plumage and a white throat. Male and female look the same.

Voice: The great horned's 4 to 6 deep hoots—*whoo-whoo-whoo-whoo-whoo*—can be heard throughout the year but are most common in fall and winter.

Behavior: Considered the ultimate predator by many wildlife biologists, the great horned owl has extremely sensitive hearing and swoops down on its prey on silent wings, attacking with powerful talons.

Habitat: Deep forests, second-growth forests, deserts, and rural areas, as well as small towns throughout North America.

Natural food: A variety of prey— skunks, rats, weasels, domestic cats, large snakes, squirrels, chipmunks, woodchucks, rabbits, game birds (such as pheasants, grouse, and waterfowl), and other birds of prey (including other species of owl).

Nest: No native species nests earlier than the great horned owl, which begins in February (earlier in the South, later in northern areas). A pair may use the large nest of a hawk, eagle, crow, or heron or a large tree cavity, stump, or rock ledge as their nest site. The 2 dull white eggs require about 30 days of incubation, mostly by the female. The youngsters do not leave the nest for at least 2 months after hatching.

How to attract: These owls will live in any backyard with mature habitat that supports a variety of other wildlife, especially a grove of tall conifers. Their presence is most noticeable at night, when they hoot.

Chimney Swift *Chaetura pelagica*

Winter
Breeding
All year

Identification: Its bow-shaped wings are the signature of the 5-inch chimney swift, the only swift east of the Mississippi River. Both male and female are dark gray with lighter throats.

Voice: The chimney swift emits a series of loud, high-pitched chipperings as it flutters overhead.

Behavior: Rarely seen perched or at its nest, the chimney swift is almost always observed flying above cities and suburbs on summer evenings. In winter, the entire population migrates to the Amazon River basin.

Habitat: Formerly hollow trees and caves, but nowadays the open air above cities, towns, villages, and farms—anywhere chimneys are available.

Natural food: Insects caught during flight.

Nest: As its name suggests, the chimney swift nests in chimneys— and in air shafts, attics, silos, and old wells. The nest of twigs is attached to the wall with the bird's own saliva (like the nest of the related Asian swift of bird's-nest soup fame). The 4 or 5 pure white oval eggs are incubated by both parents, sometimes at the same time, for 18 to 21 days. Young fly when they are a month old, but they may return to the nest to roost.

How to attract: Any urban or suburban chimney within the chimney swift's range is a potential nesting site.

Ruby-throated Hummingbird *Archilochus colubris*

Identification: Of the 15 species of hummingbirds breeding in the United States and Canada, only the ruby-throated nests east of the Great Plains. Male and female alike are 3- to 3½-inch flying jewels with iridescent metallic green bodies and long, needle-sharp bills. The fork-tailed male sports a fiery red iridescent throat; the female is gray white below and has a blunted tail.

Voice: Both sexes utter high-pitched, squeaky chippering calls and make buzzing noises with their wings. Males buzz during pendulum-patterned courtship flights.

Behavior: Like all hummingbirds, ruby-throats spend a great deal of time on the wing, buzzing here and there in search of flowers containing nectar. When they do shut down their motors, they often perch inconspicuously on tree branches.

Habitat: Gardens surrounded by woodland, orchards, or shade trees.

Natural food: Mostly flower nectar; also tiny insects and spiders.

Nest: The tiny cup-shaped nest is attached with spider silk to a small twig or branch 6 to 50 feet above ground level. Lined with plant down, the nest usually contains 2 white eggs the size of navy beans. The female incubates the eggs for 14 to 16 days, and the young leave the nest at about 3 weeks of age.

How to attract: Any garden east of the Great Plains that contains brightly colored, nectar-producing flowers (such as coral bells, fuchsia, or honeysuckle—also see page 79) and is surrounded by trees should attract ruby-throats. They also drink sugar water (see page 92).

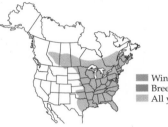

Winter
Breeding
All year

Black-chinned Hummingbird *Archilochus alexandri*

Identification: A black chin above a bluish purple throat distinguishes the male of the black-chinned hummingbird species. Both sexes of this 3½-inch bird are metallic green above; the female is white below. The male's tail is notched.

Voice: The male black-chinned hummingbird sings a soft, high-pitched *chew*. When chasing other hummers, it also makes a loud chippering sound.

Behavior: Like the ruby-throated hummingbird, its close relative, the black-chinned male courts females with a dramatic pendulum flight, sometimes tracing a figure 8.

Habitat: Semiarid canyons and woodlands near streams, lowlands, and parks of the West.

Natural food: The pollen and nectar of arid tree flowers and garden blossoms; also insects captured by darting out from a tree perch.

Nest: Typically, the black-chin builds its small, cup-shaped nest 4 to 8 feet above the ground in a tree or shrub. The nesting material is white or buff plant down overed with spider silk. The 2 pure white eggs are incubated by the female for about 16 days. The young leave the nest about 3 weeks after hatching, but they are still fed by the female. Two or 3 broods a year are common.

How to attract: Western gardens with native plants producing small, bright-colored, nectar-filled flowers should attract black-chinned hummingbirds. Surrounding woodlands draw them, as does sugar water.

Winter
Breeding
All year

Anna's Hummingbird *Calypte anna*

Winter
Breeding
All year

Identification: Among the most spectacular of North American hummingbirds, the 4-inch male Anna's has a jewel-like metallic green body punctuated with a brilliant rose cap and throat. The female lacks the bright top but usually has some rose-colored feathers in the throat.

Voice: The male Anna's sings a series of thin, squeaky notes from a tree perch or while in a courtship flight. Both sexes chirp while feeding from blossoms.

Behavior: The Anna's is the only hummingbird that often winters in the United States. During the summer breeding season, the female may build a new nest, lay eggs, and begin to incubate while still feeding youngsters from the previous brood.

Habitat: Chaparral, mixed woodland, parks, and gardens of the Pacific Coast and the Southwest.

Natural food: Insects (a greater portion than for most other hummingbirds), bleeding tree sap from sapsucker drillings, and the nectar of tree blossoms and garden flowers.

Nest: Somewhat large for a hummingbird nest, the Anna's cup of plant down covered with spider silk and lichens is built on a branch as high as 30 feet above the ground. The 2 white eggs are incubated by the female for 16 days before hatching. Youngsters fly away in about 3 weeks.

How to attract: Sugar-water feeders in a flower garden featuring such nectar-filled blooms as bee balm, coral bells, and honeysuckle, surrounded by natural habitat, should attract the Anna's (see pages 79 and 92).

Broad-tailed Hummingbird *Selasphorus platycercus*

Winter
Breeding
All year

Identification: Similar in appearance to the ruby-throated of the East, the 4½-inch male broad-tailed hummingbird has a rose red throat, white belly, and metallic green body. The female is green above with a speckled throat and reddish brown flanks and belly.

Voice: The call of the broad-tail is a sharp *chip*, but a more characteristic noise is the loud, musical, cricketlike buzzing sound made by the male's wings while in flight.

Behavior: Like all other hummingbirds, the broad-tail is an incredible flier, zipping up and down, back and forth, or hanging motionless in mid-air while its wings beat in a blur.

Habitat: Forests of piñon and juniper, canyons, and gardens in the Rocky Mountain region at elevations of 4,000 to 11,000 feet.

Natural food: The nectar and insects found on and around high-country vegetation.

Nest: The broad-tailed hummingbird builds its nest 3 to 20 feet above the ground on a horizontal branch of a tree or shrub. Tree down forms the outer walls of the cup, which is decorated with shreds of bark, fine leaves, and lichen. The 2 white eggs are incubated by the female for 16 days. The young are on the wing at about 3 weeks of age.

How to attract: The broad-tail sips nectar from red geraniums, penstemons, lupines, petunias, and other bright flowers (especially native). It drinks sugar water and is attracted in summer to hummingbird feeders in gardens (see pages 79 and 92).

Belted Kingfisher *Ceryle alcyon*

Identification: In most of North America, the 13-inch belted kingfisher is the only member of the kingfisher tribe to be seen. Both male and female have large heads with ragged crests and large, sharp bills. Both have a slate blue back and band across a white breast. Females also have a robin-red breast band below.

Voice: Rattling is the best way to describe the loud call of a belted kingfisher.

Behavior: When fishing, belted kingfishers watch for prey from perches or hover above water until they spot a fish, then dive into the water, bill first, creating a mighty splash. A catch is flown to a nearby perch to be swallowed whole, head first.

Habitat: Along the shores of lakes, ponds, and streams where it can fish and nest.

Natural food: Almost entirely small fish, though the belted kingfisher may also prey on crayfish, crabs, frogs, snakes, and insects.

Nest: Belted kingfishers usually nest at the end of a 3- to 6-foot-long burrow excavated in a bank near water. Incubation of the 6 or 7 pure white eggs is shared by both parents for 23 or 24 days. The young leave the burrow 3 to 4 weeks after they hatch.

How to attract: People who live on or near water can place a perch at the water's edge from which the birds can fish. (Watch out—they may rob your goldfish pond.)

Winter
Breeding
All year

Red-headed Woodpecker *Melanerpes erythrocephalus*

Identification: A totally red head is the main distinguishing feature of both the male and female red-headed woodpecker. This bird is very showy in flight as its black and white back, wings, and tail ripple through the woodland.

Voice: Its distinctive *queeah, queeah, queeah* call is often heard before this bird is seen.

Behavior: The introduction of the European starling in North America in the late 19th century created unnatural competition for nesting cavities. That and loss of habitat have made the species scarce in the northeastern United States.

Habitat: Mature woodlands of both coniferous and deciduous forests, wooded farmland, and city parks and gardens in the eastern United States.

Natural food: Half animal matter, the other half tree nuts and the fruits of trees, shrubs, and vines. Though the red-headed doesn't drill trees for food as much as other woodpeckers do, it does forage on the ground for insects, ants, spiders, grubs, wasps, and beetles.

Nest: Both sexes share excavation of their 8- to 24-inch-deep nesting cavity, usually 8 to 80 feet above the ground in a live or dead tree, utility pole, or fence post. The 5 pure white eggs are incubated by both parents for about 14 days.

How to attract: If you have a backyard or garden with mature trees nearby, offer suet and birdseed to attract this colorful woodpecker. It may nest in a birdhouse (6 by 6 by 14 inches high with a 2-inch hole) erected 12 to 20 feet above the ground. Dead trees provide nest sites, too.

Winter
Breeding
All year

Red-bellied Woodpecker   *Melanerpes carolinus*

Winter
Breeding
All year

Identification: The zebra-backed, 9-inch male red-bellied woodpecker has a bright red crown and nape, a white rump, and white patches on the outer wings. The female is similar, but only her nape is red. Red-bellied woodpeckers do have a reddish wash on the lower belly, but it is difficult to see.

Voice: The distinct *yuk* call of the red-bellied woodpecker, once learned, is easily recognized. It also calls a series of *chuf-chuf-chuf-chuf* notes.

Behavior: Originally a southeastern species, the red-bellied remains east of the Mississippi but has extended its range into New England and the upper Midwest, thanks in part to the availability of feeding stations.

Habitat: Forests, orchards, gardens, and backyards with mature trees.

Natural food: Wood-boring insects, beetles, crickets, and flies; acorns and other nuts that may be cached for winter use. Citrus fruits and juice are favorites, too.

Nest: Male and female work to dig a nesting cavity 5 to 70 feet above the ground in a tree, utility pole, or building. The 4 or 5 pure white eggs are incubated by both parents for 14 days. The young are on the wing in 3½ weeks.

How to attract: Suet, sunflower seeds, and cracked corn will attract this woodpecker. It may use a birdhouse (6 by 6 by 14 inches high with a 2½-inch hole) placed 12 to 20 feet above the ground. Dead trees provide nest sites, too.

Yellow-bellied Sapsucker   *Sphyrapicus varius*

Winter
Breeding
All year

Identification: A multicolored woodpecker, the 8-inch yellow-bellied sapsucker has a bright red forehead, black and white head, long white wing bar, and black barred back. Its yellowish belly has some speckling. The male has a red throat, the female a white throat. In some regions, the yellow-bellied (like its close relatives in the West, the red-naped and red-breasted sapsuckers) is distinguished by more red on the head.

Voice: A nasal *mew* and the alarm cry *churr-churr-churr* are common calls of this species.

Behavior: This sapsucker doesn't actually suck sap, but the holes it drills in trees make the sap run, enabling the bird to lap it up with its brushlike tongue. The sapsucker keeps returning to these holes, harvesting insects that are also attracted to the sap.

Habitat: Coniferous or deciduous forests, or wooded groves around homes and gardens.

Natural food: The sap of trees and the insects attracted to the sap, as well as other woodland insects.

Nest: A nesting cavity 10 to 12 inches deep is excavated by both male and female in a live or dead tree, 5 to 30 feet above the ground. On the average, 4 eggs are incubated by both parents (the male at night) for 11 or 12 days. The youngsters leave in about a month.

How to attract: Yellow-bellied sapsuckers love suet. They also relish the sugar water in hummingbird feeders (see page 92). They like to drill holes in deciduous fruit trees.

Downy Woodpecker   *Picoides pubescens*

Identification: The male downy is a little black and white woodpecker with a single red spot on the back of its head. The female lacks the red spot. This 6-inch bird has a short bill, and its plumage has a "downy" appearance.

Voice: A high-pitched whinny is the location call of this little woodpecker, and a contented *pik* describes its call while feeding.

Behavior: During winter, both sexes begin drumming on trees to establish nesting territories. Courting takes place in late winter, when the pair dances around tree branches, wings raised in tempo with the couple's chattering.

Habitat: Open woodland of mixed growth, orchards, swamps, riverbanks, and wooded backyards.

Natural food: Wood-boring insects, insect eggs, and cocoons; also fruits, weed seeds, and crop grains. Clinging to a tree, a downy pecks with jerking movements to scale away loose bark in search of food.

Nest: The female does most of the work to excavate the nest, an 8- to 10-inch-deep tree cavity 3 to 50 feet above the ground. The 4 or 5 white eggs are incubated by both parents (the male at night) for 12 days, and the young are on the wing in about 3 weeks.

How to attract: Of all the woodpeckers, the downy is the most common visitor to backyards—especially those with fruit trees—across the continent. It is fond of suet but will also eat cracked sunflower seeds and corn. Dead trees provide nest sites.

Winter
Breeding
All year

Hairy Woodpecker   *Picoides villosus*

Identification: Except for its larger size, the 9-inch hairy woodpecker is a near copy of the black and white downy (above). Its bill is also proportionately larger and more chiseled than that of the downy. The hairy is named for the bristlelike feathers around its bill.

Voice: The hairy's whinny is deeper and faster than the downy's, and its *peek* call is louder and more metallic.

Behavior: Hairy woodpeckers are much shyer than downies. Once they settle on a breeding territory, the pair is likely to remain there for the rest of their lives.

Habitat: Coniferous and deciduous forests, swamps, and orchards, including backyards that have mature trees.

Natural food: The larvae of wood-boring insects (more than 75 percent of the hairy's diet). It is believed that this woodpecker can actually hear or feel the insects with its bill when it pecks into a tree.

Nest: Hairy woodpeckers build a new nesting cavity each year, 10 to 12 inches deep and 5 to 30 feet above the ground, often in a tree with a decayed center. The 4 white eggs are incubated by both sexes (the male at night) for 11 or 12 days. Young birds are out of the cavity in about a month.

How to attract: Suet is the major food for attracting hairy woodpeckers to backyards and gardens, but they will also eat sunflower seeds, corn, and scraps of meat and fruit. Dead trees provide nest sites.

Winter
Breeding
All year

Northern Flicker *Colaptes auratus*

Winter
Breeding
All year

Identification: The 12-inch flicker is a large woodpecker with a brown striped back and a spotted, buff-colored belly. Both sexes have black bibs and white rumps, but only the males have mustaches—either black (in the East) or red (in the West). Regional forms also vary in the color of their wing feather shafts—yellow in the East or red in the West—differences which show up best in flight. Eastern flickers of both sexes have a red chevron on the nape, lacking in western birds.

Voice: Flickers are loud birds, and their rhythmic call—*ka-ka-ka-ka*—often can be heard at a great distance.

Behavior: Northern flickers are unique among the woodpeckers in that they feed on the ground rather than in trees.

Habitat: Open deciduous and coniferous forests, orchards, roadsides, and backyard lawns.

Natural food: Ants and other ground-inhabiting insects, procured by means of the flicker's long, sticky tongue; also fruit, berries, and weed seeds.

Nest: Flickers nest in tree cavities 2 to 60 feet above the ground; both sexes help excavate the nest to a depth of 10 to 36 inches. Their 6 to 8 white eggs are incubated for 11 or 12 days, mostly by the male. The young are out of the nest less than a month after hatching.

How to attract: Northern flickers like suet, also raisins and apples. They might nest in a 7 by 7 by 18-inch-high birdhouse with a 2½-inch hole, erected 6 to 20 feet above the ground. Dead trees provide nest sites, too.

Black Phoebe *Sayornis nigricans*

Winter
Breeding
All year

Identification: The 7-inch black phoebe looks amazingly like the dark-eyed junco (see page 56), but its erect posture and flicking tail distinguish it from the junco. Both male and female are black overall, except for a white lower belly, undertail coverts, and outer tail feathers.

Voice: The black phoebe's song is a high-pitched, plaintive *ti-wee*, sounded twice; the alarm note is a loud, sharp *tsip*.

Behavior: A bird of the shadows, the black phoebe watches for insect prey from a shaded perch, attacking from above on mothlike wings. The clicking of its bill indicates a strike.

Habitat: In the Southwest along shaded streams, on farms, and in parks and gardens, always near water.

Natural food: Insects—wasps, flies, ants, moths, and caterpillars.

Nest: The black phoebe builds its nest of mud over doors and windows, under bridges, and on cliffs, often under an overhang, sometimes near heavy human traffic, and always near water. A lining of wool, hair, feathers, or plant fibers cushions the 4 white eggs, which are incubated by the female for 15 to 17 days. Three weeks later the young can fly.

How to attract: Residents of the Southwest who have seen black phoebes nearby might place shelves above the doors or windows of their homes or other structures where the birds could nest. The moisture of a pool or damp lawn attracts them, too.

Eastern Phoebe *Sayornis phoebe*

Identification: A member of the flycatcher family, the 6½-inch eastern phoebe is dark olive above, with a slightly darker head, and whitish below. The bird always sits upright, flipping its tail.

Voice: The eastern phoebe calls its name with a distinct *fee-bee, fee-bee,* repeated over and over again.

Behavior: One of the earliest birds to migrate north to its nesting grounds in the spring, the eastern phoebe also lingers there longer in the fall.

Habitat: Near man-made structures close to water in ravines, around cliffs, and in suburban areas.

Natural food: Almost entirely insects, usually caught in flight.

Nest: Phoebes build a large nest on a shelflike projection over a window, on rafters of a barn or outbuilding, or on bridge girders. The 4½-inch nest of weeds, grasses, plant fibers, and mud is covered with moss and lined with hair. Five white eggs, on the average, are incubated by the female for 15 or 16 days. The young leave 2 to 3 weeks later. Two broods a year are common. Brown-headed cowbirds frequently remove phoebe eggs and replace them in the nest with their own.

How to attract: Build a shelf over the window or door of a cabin or cottage in an area inhabited by phoebes, and the birds are likely to nest there. A pond or small lake will attract them, too.

Winter
Breeding
All year

Purple Martin *Progne subis*

Identification: At 8 inches, the purple martin is the largest of the American swallows. The male is glossy blue black overall and has a forked tail. Females and immature birds are duller above, with gray bellies and mottled throats.

Voice: With wings outstretched, the purple martin calls a harsh *keerp*. Its song is a gurgling, liquid sound ending with a series of guttural notes.

Behavior: Colonies of purple martins return every spring on or about the same date to the place where they hatched. An advance guard of several males is joined a few days later by the main flock.

Habitat: Open areas near water—on farms, in cities, and in suburbs—where they can swoop down from their houses to feed on insects.

Natural food: Insects, including mosquitos and dragonflies.

Nest: Since Indians hollowed out gourds for purple martins, the birds have been nesting in man-made houses. Today, many thousands of multiple-room martin houses are erected on lawns and in gardens across the continent. Only in the West do the birds occasionally still nest in natural cavities. Each pair produces 4 or 5 white eggs, which the female incubates for 15 or 16 days; the young are ready to fly in about a month.

How to attract: Purple martins may be enticed to move into a multiple-room martin house erected 15 to 20 feet above ground on a pole in an open area near water. Dead trees provide nest sites, too.

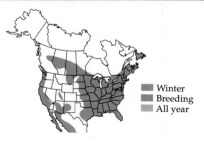

Winter
Breeding
All year

33B Purple Martin

Tree Swallow   *Tachycineta bicolor*

Winter
Breeding
All year

Identification: The first swallow species to move north in the spring, the handsome 5- to 6-inch tree swallow is steely blue green above and white below. Male and female are similar, but females are much browner than males. Young tree swallows are brown gray above and white below with a shaded breast band.

Voice: The liquid twittering song of the tree swallow is a pleasant chatter. In flight, the bird will call *silip*.

Behavior: Unlike some other swallows, tree swallows are not colonial birds and usually nest in isolated pairs. They do flock during migration, however, when their numbers can be impressive.

Habitat: Wooded swamps or open fields near water, but often close to humans.

Natural food: Mostly insects taken in flight while the bird courses over water or fields; some weed seeds and fruit as well.

Nest: Tree swallows are cavity nesters and will use birdhouses, mailboxes, woodpecker holes, and fence posts as nesting sites. The nest itself is an accumulation of grasses lined with feathers. The 4 to 6 pure white eggs are incubated for 13 to 16 days by the female. Young leave the nest in about 3 weeks, or whenever conditions are favorable.

How to attract: Tree swallows will readily nest in birdhouses (5 by 5 by 6 inches high, with a 1½-inch diameter hole); place them 10 to 15 feet high on posts near water.

Violet-green Swallow   *Tachycineta thalassina*

Winter
Breeding
All year

Identification: The male violet-green swallow has a brilliant green back and purple rump, white belly, and notched tail. The female is browner above, and young birds are gray. Similar to the tree swallow, this 5½-inch western species has more white on its flanks, nearly meeting over the tail and also surrounding the eye.

Voice: Violet-green swallows twitter a great deal while in flight. The male will sing *tsip-tseet-tsip* while courting.

Behavior: A bird that seems to enjoy flying high, this swallow chatters as it flutters in search of insects.

Habitat: Open woodland along the Pacific coast and at higher elevations in the mountains, north to Alaska.

Natural food: Insects taken on the wing, often at great heights.

Nest: Though they frequently nest in single pairs, violet-greens will sometimes nest near tree swallows, bluebirds, nuthatches, woodpeckers, and wrens in wooded areas where there are lots of holes. They build their nests in natural cavities, old woodpecker holes, cliffs, or birdhouses, using dried grasses and feathers as lining. The 4 or 5 oval white eggs are incubated by the female for 13 or 14 days. The young fly 10 days after hatching but may return to the nest to roost.

How to attract: If you live in the West near water, you may be able to attract violet-green swallows by erecting a birdhouse (5 by 5 by 6 inches high with a 1½-inch diameter hole) 10 to 15 feet above the ground on a post.

Barn Swallow *Hirundo rustica*

Identification: The classic swallow of Europe, the barn swallow is the most common and best-known member of its family in North America. Both male and female are metallic blue black above and cinnamon below, with darker reddish brown throat. A deeply forked tail is the most distinct feature. Young barn swallows are paler below and have shorter tails.

Voice: The barn swallow constantly chatters, using a variety of harsh notes strung together.

Behavior: Barn swallows are superb fliers, constantly making aerial adjustments as they search for insects and court mates. Barn swallows bathe and drink while skimming ponds and lakes.

Habitat: Barns, natural caves, outbuildings, bridges, and other structures on farms and in suburbs.

Natural food: Insects taken on the wing over cultivated fields, meadows, barnyards, and ponds.

Nest: These colonial birds often plaster their mud nests to rafters or beams of barns, bridges, or boathouses. After lining the nest with soft feathers, they lay 4 or 5 brown-spotted white eggs. Both parents incubate the eggs, sometimes alternating every 15 minutes, for 15 days. The female sits on the eggs at night while the male remains nearby. The young fly in about 3 weeks.

How to attract: Aside from building a barn, there isn't much you can do to encourage barn swallows to nest nearby. They seem to adopt people; people don't adopt them. They do love ponds and need mud for their nests.

Winter
Breeding
All year

Steller's Jay *Cyanocitta stelleri*

Identification: The blue-crested jay of the West, the Steller's is a 12-inch bird with dark blue wings and tail, black markings on the head, upper back, and breast, and inconspicuous white streaks on the face. Male and female look alike.

Voice: This is a loud bird, squawking *waah, waah, waah* and *shook, shook, shook;* but during courtship, the male whispers his song to his mate. The Steller's mimics the voices of the red-shouldered and red-tailed hawks.

Behavior: Often shy in deep forests, the Steller's can be bold at campsites and picnic grounds. Though it may travel in flocks of a dozen or more, it is less gregarious than other jays (but more so than the scrub jay).

Habitat: Western coniferous forests and mixed oak/pine woodlands.

Natural food: Acorns and pine seeds that may be hoarded for winter consumption; also insects, carrion, and camp leftovers. The Steller's sometimes raids the stores of acorns from woodpeckers and steals the caches of other jays.

Nest: Steller's jays build their bulky nests in trees, usually conifers, 8 to 40 feet above the ground. The foundation of dry leaves, moss, and trash, mixed with mud, is lined with rootlets and pine needles. The 4 pale greenish eggs, spotted with brown, are incubated primarily by the female for 17 or 18 days. Parents are quiet when near their nest, but they protest loudly if discovered.

How to attract: Steller's jays like the moist shade of conifers; birdseed and suet are favorite foods.

Winter
Breeding
All year

Blue Jay *Cyanocitta cristata*

Winter
Breeding
All year

Identification: The only blue-crested jay of the East, this striking 11-inch bird is bright blue above with white on wings and tail and light gray below. Both sexes look alike.

Voice: The blue jay's demanding *jay, jay, jay* can be heard at some distance. Its bell-like *too-lee, too-lee* call is softer. The male's whisper song is for his mate. Blue jays mimic the red-shouldered and red-tailed hawks.

Behavior: The blue jay is aggressive and crafty. During courtship, several males will chase a single female until she selects one of them as a mate.

Habitat: Forests, farms, parks, and the backyards and gardens of suburbs and cities of the eastern United States.

Natural food: Acorns and other tree seeds and nuts; also grains, fruits, insects, fish, salamanders, sometimes small birds, and eggs in nests.

Nest: Blue jays build bulky nests, from 5 to 50 feet above the ground, that are well hidden in thickets, frequently near houses. Both male and female gather sticks, twigs, bark, and leaves for the nest and then line it with rootlets; both incubate their 4 or 5 eggs, olive or buff-colored with dark brown spots, for 17 or 18 days. The youngsters can fly in about 3 weeks.

How to attract: Just offer sunflower seeds and other birdseeds along with water and suet.

Scrub Jay *Aphelocoma coerulescens*

Winter
Breeding
All year

Identification: A crestless blue jay. that lives in both Florida and the West, the 11-inch scrub jay has a blue head, wings, and tail, a white throat outlined in blue, and a white belly.

Voice: The scrub jay utters a harsh *sheek, sheek, sheek.* The male also whispers a song to his mate.

Behavior: Scrub jays hoard food and any bright, shiny objects they find—silverware, for instance, or pieces of glass or jewelry. Florida scrub jays are often fearless around human beings, even at their nests.

Habitat: In Florida, scrub oak; in the West, oak woodland, deciduous forests, chaparral, canyons, and stream bottomland.

Natural food: Acorns, pine nuts, other tree seeds, grains, fruits, insects, and snails, and the eggs and young of small birds. Scrub jays spend much of their time foraging on the ground.

Nest: In both Florida and the West, the scrub jay nests fairly low, 3 to 30 feet above the ground, in bushes and trees. The nest is a well-constructed platform of twigs, moss, and dry grass lined with hair and rootlets. The 3 or 4 greenish eggs are marked with brown spots; the female incubates them for 16 days. Young leave the nest at 2 to 3 weeks of age.

How to attract: Scrub jays will come for suet, birdseed, bread, kitchen scraps, dog and cat food, and unshelled peanuts.

American Crow *Corvus brachyrhynchos*

Identification: The 18-inch American crow is entirely black. Even its bill and feet are black. Its tail is squared.

Voice: The hoarse *caw, caw, caw* of the American crow is a familiar sound on farms across the continent. Young crows in the nest are noisy, with a more nasal call.

Behavior: Considered among the most intelligent of all birds, the American crow can learn quickly and is able to communicate complicated information to its fellow crows.

Habitat: Forests, farmlands, wooded lots, and suburban areas with mature trees.

Natural food: Nearly anything—carrion on highways, fish, earthworms, insects, and the eggs and young of other birds, as well as fruit, grains, and garbage.

Nest: Solitary nesters, a pair of American crows will usually build their large, basketlike nest of sticks near the trunk or crotch of a tree, 10 to 70 feet above the ground. The nest is lined with shredded bark fibers, moss, feathers, fur, hair, roots, or leaves. The pair's 4 to 6 bluish or grayish green eggs marked with brown spots are incubated by both parents for 18 days. Young fly when they are about a month old.

How to attract: Most people would not try to attract crows—but crows will come for suet and birdseed.

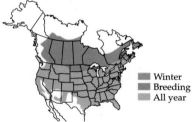

Winter
Breeding
All year

Black-capped Chickadee *Parus atricapillus*

Identification: A gray and black ball of fluff weighing just a third of an ounce—that's the black-capped chickadee. Gray above and whitish below, this 5-inch bird is distinguished by a distinct black cap, black bib, white cheek marks, buff-colored flanks, and a long tail. Male and female look alike.

Voice: A more definitive identification of the black-capped chickadee might be the *chick-a-dee-dee-dee* call, or the male's springtime *phee-bee* song.

Behavior: This active, curious, and quick-moving bird can change directions in midair in 3/100th of a second. It is also among the tamest of all backyard species and can be trained to eat from the hand.

Habitat: Deciduous and coniferous forests as well as rural woodland and suburban backyards in the northern United States.

Natural food: The eggs and larvae of tree-inhabiting insects; also fruit and seeds.

Nest: Both sexes excavate the 5- to 8-inch nesting cavity in rotting wood, 4 to 10 feet above the ground. During the 12 to 13 days that the female incubates their 6 to 8 eggs (white with reddish brown spots), the male feeds her. Both parents feed the young during the 2-week nesting period.

How to attract: Black-capped chickadees love sunflower seeds. They may nest in a birdhouse (4 by 4 by 10 inches high with a 1¼-inch entrance hole) placed 6 to 15 feet above the ground, or will also nest in dead trees. They like coniferous shrubs and trees.

Winter
Breeding
All year

Carolina Chickadee   *Parus carolinensis*

Winter
Breeding
All year

Identification: Similar to the black-capped chickadee but smaller, the 4½-inch Carolina has a shorter black bib, less white on its wings, and a shorter tail. Both sexes look alike.

Voice: The Carolina's *chick-a-dee-dee-dee* call is faster and higher-pitched than that of the black-capped; its *phee-bee* song is four notes instead of two.

Behavior: The Carolina chickadee keeps to woodland areas and is attached to its southeastern home range.

Habitat: The rural woodland and coniferous forests of the Southeast, from the coastal lowlands to altitudes of 4,000 feet.

Natural food: Insects and their eggs and larvae; also seeds and fruits gleaned from the woodlands of the Southeast.

Nest: A 5- to 6-inch hole some 5 or 6 feet above the ground is excavated by the nesting pair in soft or rotted wood over a 2-week period. They may also use an abandoned woodpecker hole or birdhouse. The nest is lined with moss, animal hair, feathers, and plant down. The 6 white eggs, spotted with brown, are incubated by the female for 13 days while the male brings her food.

How to attract: Offer sunflower seeds, suet, and peanut butter mix, and erect a birdhouse (4 by 4 by 10 inches high with a 1¼-inch entrance hole) placed 5 feet above the ground. Evergreens are appreciated for cover.

Tufted Titmouse   *Parus bicolor*

Winter
Breeding
All year

Identification: The 6-inch tufted titmouse is a mouselike bird with a gray crest, buff-colored flanks, and beady black eyes. In the West, it is replaced by the plain titmouse. Male and female look alike.

Voice: The tufted titmouse's familiar *pet-tow, pet-tow, pet-tow* brightens any woodland. Its *day-day-day* alarm note sounds harsher and more demanding.

Behavior: This species has extended its range into the Northeast and upper Midwest and is usually in the company of chickadees and nuthatches as it forages noisily through woodland.

Habitat: Backyards and gardens; also forests, swamps, and orchards of the East.

Natural food: A variety of insects, their eggs, and larvae, as well as seeds and fruit found in the woods. With its sharp, black bill, the tufted titmouse opens moth cocoons for the larva inside.

Nest: Like chickadees, the tufted titmouse nests inside a tree cavity, often taking over one hollowed out by a woodpecker. The 5 or 6 speckled and creamy eggs are incubated for 13 or 14 days by the female; the male calls her out of the cavity to feed her. The young leave the nest 17 or 18 days after hatching.

How to attract: Titmice are fond of sunflower seeds, and they relish suet on cold days. Occasionally they'll use a birdhouse (4 by 4 by 10 inches high with a 1¼-inch entrance hole) placed 6 to 15 feet above the ground. They may be attracted to oak trees.

Bushtit   *Psaltriparus minimus*

Identification: A tiny, dull gray bird with a brown cap, long tail, and very short bill, the 3½-inch bushtit is the smallest member of the North American titmouse family. Both sexes look alike except for their eyes—dark brown for males (and young birds), cream-colored for females.

Voice: Bushtits are constantly vocal to keep flocks together, uttering *tsit-tsit-tsit* as they feed. They have no song.

Behavior: Bushtits are even more active than chickadees and titmice. Except during the breeding season, they are found in flocks numbering as few as a half dozen or as many as 50, foraging through the thickets with other small birds.

Habitat: Forest thickets, oak woodland, chaparral, canyons, and streamsides in the West.

Natural food: Insects, insect eggs, and larvae; also fruits and seeds.

Nest: Male and female work together to weave a 6- to 8-inch gourd-shaped basket nest over a 13- to 51-day period. Located 6 to 35 feet above the ground in a bush or tree, the nest is lined with mosses, lichens, leaves, and spider silk. Both parents spend nights in the nest while incubating the 5 to 7 white eggs for 12 or 13 days. The young fly at about 2 weeks of age.

How to attract: Bushtits may come to sunflower seeds and suet, but are most apt to appear near ponds and thick evergreen shrubs in sunny areas.

Winter
Breeding
All year

Red-breasted Nuthatch   *Sitta canadensis*

Identification: The stubby little red-breasted nuthatch is a 4½-inch acrobat with a gray back, rusty breast, black cap, white eye line, and short tail. Like other nuthatches, it hops down the tree head first.

Voice: The song of this species is a trumpetlike *wea-wea-wea-wea*. Its alarm call is a more disturbed *tank-tank-tank-tank*.

Behavior: A species of the northern woods country, the red-breasted nuthatch may move south in great numbers during winters, when its natural foods are scarce. At the entrance to its nesting cavity in a dead or rotted tree, the red-breasted nuthatch dabs pine resin or pitch to discourage predators from entering. Sometimes the red-breasted nuthatch gets stuck, too.

Habitat: Northern coniferous forests, but in winter also backyards and gardens across the continent.

Natural food: The seeds of pines, firs, and spruce, mixed with a diet of insects, insect eggs, and larvae.

Nest: The red-breasted nuthatch builds its nest 4 inches into an excavated tree cavity—sometimes a woodpecker hole. The nest is lined with mosses, grasses, and feathers to protect the 5 or 6 reddish-spotted white eggs. The female incubates the eggs for 12 days; the young fly about 3 weeks after hatching.

How to attract: Sunflower seeds and suet are favorite foods. Conifers will attract red-breasted nuthatches, too (they rarely use birdhouses).

Winter
Breeding
All year

White-breasted Nuthatch   *Sitta carolinensis*

Winter
Breeding
All year

Identification: The white-breasted nuthatch is a 6-inch blue gray bird with a black cap, white breast and belly, and stubby tail. It moves down tree trunks head first.

Voice: The white-breasted's song is a series of rapid whistles—*whit-whi-whit-whi-whi*. Its alarm note is a loud, harsh *yank, yank, yank*, slower and more nasal than the red-breasted's.

Behavior: White-breasted nuthatches often forage in the woods in the company of chickadees, titmice, and brown creepers. These "upside-down birds" can see food in bark crevices that birds coming up the tree trunk might miss.

Habitat: Mixed woodland, orchards, and mature trees in suburbs and cities.

Natural food: Nuts and seeds in fall and winter; also insects in spring and summer. The white-breasted wedges tree nuts and seeds into crevices in the tree bark to hammer them open with its bill; as a result, the bird was first called "nut-hack."

Nest: A white-breasted nuthatch pair nests in a tree cavity (often in a woodpecker hole) 15 to 50 feet above the ground. The female lines the nest with bark shreds, twigs, grass, fur, and hair. Then she lays 8 white eggs, heavily marked with light brown spots, and incubates them for 12 days. Youngsters can fly in 2 weeks.

How to attract: One of the most common of all backyard and garden species in the East and Midwest, the white-breasted nuthatch relishes sunflower seeds and suet.

Brown Creeper   *Certhia americana*

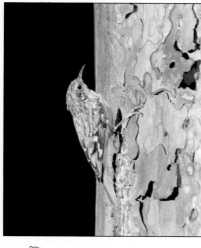

Winter
Breeding
All year

Identification: Nearly invisible against tree bark, the 5-inch brown creeper is streaked brown above and white below. It has a sharp, slightly curved bill and a long, stiff tail upon which it leans against tree trunks.

Voice: The brown creeper's single high-pitched *seee* is hardly noticeable. In spring, the male sings a high-pitched *see-see-see-sisi-see*.

Behavior: Starting at the base of a tree, the brown creeper searches for food by working its way up in a spiraling path around the tree trunk until it reaches the top. Then it flies down to the base of a nearby tree and begins a new spiral upward.

Habitat: Coniferous and deciduous forests, mixed woodland and swamps, and wooded backyards throughout the continent.

Natural food: Almost entirely insects that it sweeps from tree trunks.

Nest: Not really a cavity nester, the brown creeper hides its nest behind a loose slab of bark 5 to 15 feet above the ground. The nest is made of leaves, twigs, and bark shreds and is lined with finer bark shreds, grass, and moss. Both sexes incubate the 5 or 6 peppered white eggs for 14 or 15 days. The young spend that much more time in the nest after hatching.

How to attract: Though brown creepers seem to like suet, they are really interested in the tiny insects that the suet attracts. They also come to conifers and big dead trees.

Carolina Wren   *Thryothorus ludovicianus*

Identification: The largest wren in the East, the 5½-inch Carolina is rich brown above a buff belly, with a white throat, tawny sides, and a conspicuous white eye line.

Voice: The Carolina's hearty *tea-kettle, tea-kettle, tea-kettle* is one of the definitive sounds of the South. Its alarm note is a buzzing noise that sounds like a thumb being rubbed against the teeth of a comb.

Behavior: Though its conspicuous song is bold, the Carolina is retiring, hiding itself in the deep tangles and brush of southeastern woodlands. Pioneers of this species have tried, with limited success, to expand its range northward into New England and the upper Midwest.

Habitat: Brushy thickets and hedges and the tangles of suburban gardens in the East.

Natural food: Primarily insects, but also snails, small frogs, lizards, fruits, and berries.

Nest: Like other wrens, the Carolina is a cavity nester, selecting a woodpecker hole, stone wall, or hole in an outbuilding in which to build its bulky nest of leaves, twigs, and weed stalks. The nest is lined with feathers, grass, moss, and hair. While the female incubates the 5 or 6 spotted pink eggs for 14 days, the attentive male feeds her. The young are on the wing 2 weeks after hatching.

How to attract: Carolina wrens are common visitors to backyards that offer suet cakes mixed with cornmeal, sunflower seeds, and other seeds. A birdbath also attracts them, and they seek thickets where they can hide.

Winter
Breeding
All year

House Wren   *Troglodytes aedon*

Identification: A little brown bird—that describes the plainest of all wrens, the 4½-inch house wren. The most common wren in the East, the house wren is dark brown above and light brown below, without any streaks or eye lines in either sex.

Voice: The bubbling, chattering, repetitive song of the male house wren rises and then falls at the end. The scolding note of the species is a series of *zzzzzzsssszzz* sounds.

Behavior: Arriving on the breeding grounds in the spring a week or two before the female, the male sings and builds dummy nests of sticks in several viable nesting sites. When the female arrives, she selects one of the male's nests, or builds her own in a new location, and lines it in preparation for the eggs.

Habitat: Backyards, farmland, and open forests.

Natural food: Nothing but insects, from caterpillars to grasshoppers to spiders.

Nest: Famous for where they nest—boots, car radiators, mailboxes, laundry on clotheslines—house wrens build stick nests lined with grass, plant fibers, feathers, and rubbish. In the wild, they choose a hole in a tree or other natural crevice. The 6 or 7 cinnamon-speckled white eggs are incubated for about 13 days; young leave the nest at 12 to 18 days of age.

How to attract: Among the most common backyard nesters in North America, house wrens may be lured with wren houses (4 by 4 by 6 inches high with a 1½-inch entrance hole) 6 to 10 feet above the ground. Try several in the same half-acre. Wrens also use brush, woodpiles, berry tangles, and wild areas.

Winter
Breeding
All year

Golden-crowned Kinglet *Regulus satrapa*

Winter
Breeding
All year

Identification: A tiny flit of a bird, the 3½-inch golden-crowned kinglet is olive green above and lighter below, with two white wing bars and a conspicuous crown of yellow and orange (male) or all yellow (female). Otherwise, sexes are alike.

Voice: Unless your hearing is acute, you may miss the call of the golden-crowned kinglet. The male's song is a high-pitched, descending *zee-zee-zee-zee;* the alarm note is a simple *tsee.*

Behavior: Ever flicking its wings, the little kinglet is constantly on the move, hopping from twig to twig and hovering as it feeds.

Habitat: Coniferous forests, mainly spruces, but also backyards and gardens during migrations.

Natural food: Insects plucked from the needles and cones of spruces while the bird hovers in midair.

Nest: The golden-crowned kinglet attaches a hanging oblong mass of mosses and lichens to the twigs of a horizontal spruce limb, some 6 to 60 feet above the ground, then lines it with fine bark, rootlets, and soft feathers. The 8 or 9 tiny, cream-colored eggs blotched with brown are laid in two layers in the nest and are believed to be incubated by the female alone for 14 or 15 days.

How to attract: Though golden-crowned kinglets do not eat birdseed, they associate with birds that do, including chickadees and brown creepers. They come for suet offered in a wooded area.

Ruby-crowned Kinglet *Regulus calendula*

Winter
Breeding
All year

Identification: The little ruby-crowned kinglet is an olive green birdlet with white wing bars and a white eye ring. Both sexes of this 4-inch species are alike, except for the male's ruby red crown spot—usually hidden under olive green feathers.

Voice: The song of the ruby-crowned is greatly out of proportion to its tiny size. The loud and husky notes start low and then rise high, *tee, tee, tue, tue, tue, ti-daddy, ti-daddy.* The *jee-didit* alarm note also seems loud for the size of this bird.

Behavior: Ruby-crowneds always seem nervous, flitting their wings and hovering as they move through pine and spruce thickets, often in the company of warblers during migration.

Habitat: Coniferous forests for breeding, but backyards during migration and western lowlands in winter.

Natural food: Mostly insects caught by hovering in front of pine and spruce cones and needles; also some fruit and seeds.

Nest: The deep cup nest of the ruby-crowned is well hidden underneath a horizontal spruce branch, 2 to 100 feet above the ground. It is lined with mosses, fur, and feathers. The female is completely concealed in the nest while she incubates the 7 to 9 pale buff eggs dotted reddish brown for about 12 days. Young fly from the nest in another 12 days.

How to attract: Birdbaths or other water sources attract ruby-crowned kinglets to yards and gardens during migration; suet appeals to them, too.

Eastern Bluebird   *Sialia sialis*

Identification: The 7-inch eastern bluebird male has a deep blue back, rusty red throat and breast, and white under its tail. The female is much duller. Juvenile bluebirds have spotted breasts.

Voice: The male bluebird's melodious *chur-a-lee* song is a welcome sign of spring. The shorter *chur-lee* call is uttered by both sexes.

Behavior: Though eastern bluebirds are solitary nesters, they are gregarious in the fall and winter, when they join forces to migrate and feed in flocks.

Habitat: Open country on farms, along roadside fences, in open woodland and swamps.

Natural food: Insects and seeds. Eastern bluebirds flutter from fence posts and wires to the ground when they spot food.

Nest: Unlike other thrushes, bluebirds nest in natural tree cavities, often in woodpecker holes, or in birdhouses. The carelessly arranged nest of grass holds 4 or 5 pale bluish white eggs, incubated by the female for 13 to 15 days; young leave the nest 2 to 3 weeks later. Two broods a year are common.

How to attract: Though eastern bluebirds will eat cornmeal mixed with suet and peanut butter, a better way to attract them is to put up birdhouses (5 by 5 by 8 inches high with a 1½-inch entrance hole) 5 to 10 feet above the ground in an open field.

Winter
Breeding
All year

Western Bluebird   *Sialia mexicana*

Identification: Its blue back and throat, brick red breast, and gray undertail coverts distinguish the 7-inch western bluebird male. Often the breast color extends across the shoulders and upper back. The female is duller overall. Juveniles have spotted breasts.

Voice: The male's warbling *chu-a-wee* is harsher and shorter than the song of the eastern bluebird. The *pew* call is given by both sexes.

Behavior: Western bluebirds fly to lower elevations in winter. They often compete with starlings and house sparrows for nesting sites, though they are compatible with pygmy nuthatches, northern flickers, tree swallows, and house wrens nesting in the same tree. In winter, they flock in numbers rarely over 30, often including a few yellow-rumped warblers.

Habitat: Open farmland areas, along roadside fences, and open woodland in mountain regions.

Natural food: Mostly insects; also berries and other fruits. The western bluebird can be seen darting out from a tree, fence post, or utility wire perch to catch insects on the wing.

Nest: Accompanied by the male, the female western bluebird builds a grass nest inside a tree cavity, often in an old woodpecker hole, or in a birdhouse. She lays 4 to 6 pale blue eggs and incubates them for 14 days.

How to attract: Fruit may attract western bluebirds to feeders, but they are more apt to be interested in birdhouses (5 by 5 by 8 inches deep with a 1½-inch entrance hole) erected 5 to 10 feet above the ground in open fields. Old fruit orchards appeal as nest sites, too.

Winter
Breeding
All year

Mountain Bluebird *Sialia currucoides*

Winter
Breeding
All year

Identification: Truly a "bluebird," the 7-inch sky blue mountain bluebird male is blue all over—light underneath, deeper above. The female is mostly gray, with blue only on the wings. Young birds are dark gray with spotted breasts.

Voice: The male's high-pitched warbling whistle, *tru-lee,* resembles that of the American robin. During migration and while living in winter flocks, the birds utter a *veer* note.

Behavior: This bluebird lives at elevations up to 12,000 feet during the breeding season. Nesting sites are often located among other species. At least one pair has been known to nest in a cliff swallow nest within a cliff swallow colony.

Habitat: At high altitudes in open rangeland, mountain meadows, and open wooded parkland.

Natural food: The mountain bluebird hovers over grasslands or darts out from rocks in pursuit of insects; also eats berries and other fruits.

Nest: Like other bluebirds, the mountain bluebird builds a grass nest in a natural cavity, often in an old woodpecker hole, but both sexes of this species contribute to the chore. The female lays 5 or 6 very pale blue eggs and then incubates them for 14 days.

How to attract: Mountain bluebirds are not likely to come to bird feeders, but they will nest in birdhouses (5 by 5 by 8 inches high with a 1½-inch entrance hole) 5 to 10 feet above the ground in an open meadow. Dead trees also provide nest sites; they like old orchards, too.

Wood Thrush *Hylocichla mustelina*

Winter
Breeding
All year

Identification: A plump thrush with a rusty red back, the 8-inch wood thrush is brighter red about the head. Its white breast is marked with large round or oval black dots. Male and female look alike.

Voice: The male wood thrush's memorable flutelike song, *gerald-deeeen,* is a magical sound of the spring woods. Both sexes call the alarm note, a rapid *pit, pit, pit.*

Behavior: Originally a bird of deep, damp forests, the wood thrush is apparently becoming more tolerant of humans; the species is nesting more frequently in garden shrubbery than in the past.

Habitat: Mostly on or near the ground in cool, wet forests, or in eastern parks and backyards that offer similar conditions.

Natural food: Insects, snails, and earthworms, as well as berries and other fruits. The wood thrush is a ground feeder.

Nest: The compact, cuplike nest is anchored about 10 feet above the ground in the crotch of a horizontal tree limb. Constructed of grass, bark, moss, paper, and mud, it is molded to fit the female wood thrush's body. She lays 3 or 4 bluish green eggs and incubates them for 13 days. When she goes away, the male guards the nest. Young fly in about 2 weeks.

How to attract: Wood thrushes may eat fruit at feeders or from berry-producing plants during the warm months. Large shrubs or small garden trees surrounded by dark woodland may attract them as nesting sites.

American Robin *Turdus migratorius*

Identification: A true thrush, the 10-inch American robin has a slate gray back and brick red breast. It also has a white eye ring, streaked white throat, and yellow bill. The male's head is a darker gray than its back; the female is paler overall. Juveniles have spotted breasts.

Voice: The male American robin carols a welcome *cheer-o-lee, cheer-o-lee, cheer-o-lee* song. Its *tut, tut, tut* alarm is demanding.

Behavior: Males return to their northern breeding grounds before the females, establishing and defending territories vigorously. In warmer regions, American robins stay all year.

Habitat: Suburban and city lawns and gardens, parks, and open wood-

land. In the West, robins may nest at altitudes up to 12,000 feet.

Natural food: Largely earthworms (located by sight, not sound); also insects, berries, and other fruits.

Nest: The American robin builds its nest in a fork or on a horizontal branch of a tree or shrub, or on a ledge, door light, or downspout. The deep cup nest of mud and grass is molded by the female's body. The 4 "robin's-egg blue" eggs are incubated by the female for 12 to 14 days, and the young leave the nest in about 2 weeks. Two broods annually are common, but rarely at the same site.

How to attract: During late spring snowstorms, American robins may eat fruit, suet, or peanut butter mix placed on or near the ground. They relish berries and fruits borne on shrubs and trees.

Winter
Breeding
All year

Gray Catbird *Dumetella carolinensis*

Identification: A slim relative of the mockingbird, the 9-inch gray catbird is gray except for a cap and long tail of black and rusty undertail coverts. Male and female look the same.

Voice: Its catlike mew gave the gray catbird its name. The song of the male is a lively series of unrelated and often disjointed musical notes and phrases. In the evening, the male may sing a quiet whisper song. The *chuck* alarm call is a scolding sound.

Behavior: The gray catbird's unimpressive appearance is more than compensated for by its many and varied calls and songs. Besides their own distinctive calls (described above), catbirds also imitate the songs of other birds and tree frog sounds, as well as some man-made noises.

Habitat: Thickets, woodland, undergrowth, hedges, and garden shrubbery.

Natural food: Insects collected on or near the ground (more than half the gray catbird's diet); also berries and other fruits.

Nest: Well concealed in a dense thicket, thick shrubbery, or briars 3 to 10 feet above the ground, the nest of the gray catbird is a bulky mass of twigs, vines, leaves, and paper built by both male and female. Deep and cuplike, the nest is lined with rootlets. The female lays 4 deep greenish blue eggs and incubates them for 12 or 13 days. The young fly at about 2 weeks.

How to attract: Catbirds may eat fruit at feeders, also from shrubs, trees, and vines. They enjoy bathing and drinking at birdbaths.

Winter
Breeding
All year

Northern Mockingbird   *Mimus polyglottos*

Winter
Breeding
All year

Identification: White wing patches and white outer tail feathers, conspicuous in flight, are distinctive field marks of an otherwise dull gray bird. Both sexes of the 10-inch northern mockingbird look alike.

Voice: Named for its creative repertoire of songs and noises—one-third its own and two-thirds mimicry—the northern mockingbird is adept at imitating both avian and man-made sounds. Even ringing alarm clocks and factory whistles are copied. Its own alarm note is a harsh *tchack*.

Behavior: Male northern mockingbirds are famous for singing at night—particularly on warm nights, it seems, when people are trying to sleep with their windows open.

Habitat: The hedges and thickets of suburban and city backyards, farmland, and brushy woodland.

Natural food: Animal matter (more than half the diet), mostly insects flushed by raising its wings in angel-like form; also berries and other fruit.

Nest: The bulky nest is concealed 3 to 10 feet above the ground in a thicket. The male suggests nesting sites by placing material, but the female has the final say. Both build. The 4 light blue green eggs, heavily blotched with brown, are incubated by the female for 12 or 13 days. Youngsters vacate the nest 10 to 12 days after hatching.

How to attract: Offer suet mixed with cornmeal and grow native berry-producing plants. Thorny species of plants offer nest sites.

Brown Thrasher   *Toxostoma rufum*

Winter
Breeding
All year

Identification: The fox red back and heavily streaked whitish breast of the 11-inch brown thrasher are conspicuous as the long-tailed bird streaks across backyards. On closer inspection, a bright yellow eye (in young birds, the iris is light blue) and down-curved bill are also evident. Both sexes look alike.

Voice: Like other members of the mockingbird tribe, the brown thrasher has a repertoire of sounds—some musical, some mechanical, most mimicked. Usually each phrase is repeated: *see it, see it; hello, hello; say what, say what*. Its alarm note is a loud *smak*.

Behavior: The male usually gives his concert from the top of a tree or shrub, head held high and long tail down.

Habitat: Thickets and hedges of suburban and city backyards and farmland.

Natural food: Insects seized by the bird's long, curved bill as it thrashes in dead leaves; also salamanders, snakes, lizards, and berries and other fruits.

Nest: Anywhere from ground level to 14 feet above in thickets, brown thrashers hide their bulky nests of twigs, grasses, and vines. Both parents incubate their 4 pale bluish white eggs (marked with fine reddish spots) for 12 or 13 days. Young leave the nest in about 2 weeks.

How to attract: Put out seeds and suet mixed with cornmeal. Low shrubs, brush piles, and berry-producing plants appeal, too.

Cedar Waxwing *Bombycilla cedrorum*

Identification: An elegant 7-inch bird of silky brown and tan with inner wing tips resembling dabs of red sealing wax, the cedar waxwing also has a yellow tip on its tail, a yellow belly, and a black mask. The two sexes look alike.

Voice: The wheezing call of the cedar waxwing is high pitched and often difficult to hear.

Behavior: If you see one bird, you almost always see a small flock of cedar waxwings. These gregarious birds remain together throughout the year, nesting in loose colonies.

Habitat: Open groves, orchards, and urban and suburban backyards, and wild areas where native berries grow.

Natural food: Insects and berries, including the berries of cedar trees and mountain ash. Cedar waxwings are known for fluttering out from trees to capture insects and for gorging themselves on berries.

Nest: These late nesters build their loosely woven nest of grass, twigs, and sometimes yarn on a horizontal branch 4 to 50 feet above the ground. Both sexes work on the nest for 5 to 7 days, finishing it with a lining of rootlets, fine grasses, and plant down. The 4 or 5 pale gray eggs with dark brown blotches are incubated by the female for 12 or 13 days. Young leave 2 to 2½ weeks after hatching.

How to attract: Water attracts cedar waxwings for drinking and bathing. You can also grow native berry-producing plants to lure them.

Winter
Breeding
All year

European Starling *Sturnus vulgaris*

Identification: Introduced 100 years ago in New York City, the 8-inch European starling has spread through most of North America. Iridescent black, green, and purple with a bright yellow bill in spring and summer, it turns speckled with a greenish bill in fall and winter. Male and female look alike.

Voice: A drawn-out whistle is its best-known sound, but the starling utters a variety of squeaks, squawks, and chatters; it will imitate the calls of other birds as well.

Behavior: The European starling has displaced many native birds from nesting cavities; the populations of eastern bluebirds, woodpeckers, and great-crested and ash-throated flycatchers have decreased as a result.

Habitat: Most often cities and suburbs, but also farmland, wooded lots, and parks, often in large flocks.

Natural food: Insects, garbage, grain, weed seeds, snails, earthworms, berries, and other fruit. Their consumption of insect pests on farms is considered beneficial, but they can damage fruit trees.

Nest: Starlings nest 10 to 25 feet above the ground in woodpecker holes, birdhouses, or any nook or cranny. Their messy collection of nesting materials ranges from grasses and twigs to feathers and trash. The 4 or 5 pale bluish green eggs are incubated by both parents for about 12 days. Young leave in about 3 weeks, are on their own a few days later.

How to attract: Starlings are generally unpopular but will come to feeders.

Winter
Breeding
All year

Red-eyed Vireo   *Vireo olivaceus*

Winter
Breeding
All year

Identification: This rather nondescript 6-inch-long bird is olive green above and white below, with a gray cap. Above the red eye is a white stripe topped with a black line. Both sexes look the same.

Voice: The male red-eyed vireo's song seems to go on and on forever with the same *See me. Here I am. Don't you see me? Here I am.* Its scolding note is a harsh, nasal *nyeah*.

Behavior: Difficult to locate in dense foliage, the red-eyed vireo throws its voice like a ventriloquist.

Habitat: Open deciduous forests of the eastern United States with thick understories of saplings.

Natural food: Insects gleaned in the foliage of deciduous trees, including some harmful to the trees. Moths and caterpillars are favorite foods.

Nest: Like the birds themselves, the cup-shaped nest is well hidden, hanging from a fork of a horizontal branch 5 to 10 feet above the ground. Using grasses, rootlets, bark strips, and paper, the female builds the nest in about 5 days, after which she lays 4 white, slightly spotted eggs and then incubates them for 12 to 14 days. In another 10 to 12 days, the young leave the nest.

How to attract: Offer moving water in a wooded backyard habitat planted with native deciduous trees.

Yellow Warbler   *Dendroica petechia*

Winter
Breeding
All year

Identification: The male yellow warbler is a 5-inch-long, bright yellow bird with an olive yellow back and red breast streaks. The female is similar but duller, lacking the streaking.

Voice: The cheerful song of the male yellow warbler is a series of *sweet, sweet, sweet* notes ending with *I'm so sweet*. The call or alarm note is a simple *chip*.

Behavior: The yellow warbler is a common victim of the brown-headed cowbird, which tosses out the warbler's eggs and replaces them in the nest with its own; but the yellow warbler simply builds more nest on top to cover the cowbird eggs. As many as six stories of nest have been found covering cowbird eggs.

Habitat: Hedges, roadside thickets, stream banks, and garden shrubbery.

Natural food: Exclusively insects, including many destructive ones, and their larvae.

Nest: Either by itself or in a loose colony, the yellow warbler builds its nest 3 to 8 feet above the ground in the upright fork of a shrub or briar. The female completes the nest in about 4 days with plant down, hair, and grasses. She lays 4 or 5 bluish white eggs with brown markings and then incubates them for 11 or 12 days. Young fly at 9 to 12 days.

How to attract: Running water will attract yellow warblers, especially near willows. They nest in multiflora roses and other thick shrubbery (in the West, where there is little deciduous forest, they depend greatly on mature streamside woods).

Pine Warbler   *Dendroica pinus*

Identification: The 5½-inch male pine warbler is olive green above and yellow on the throat and breast with dark streaks on its sides. It has prominent white wing bars, white spots on the corners of the tail, and a yellow line above each eye. Its bill is large for a warbler its size. The female is similar to the male, but duller below.

Voice: The male pine warbler's song is a musical trill on one note. The alarm call is a lisping *chip*.

Behavior: Pine warblers are among the few warbler species that remain in the United States throughout the year.

Habitat: Open pine woodland.

Natural food: Insects associated with pine woodland, supplemented with seeds, berries, and other wild fruits.

Nest: Completely hidden, the pine warbler's nest of pine needles, weed stems, bark strips, and spider webs is built 30 to 50 feet above the ground on top of a horizontal pine limb. The 4 speckled white eggs are incubated by the female—and perhaps by the male—for about 14 days.

How to attract: Groves of pine attract these birds. Also, as a popular feeding station visitor in the Southeast during the winter, the pine warbler will eat bird cakes made of suet, cornmeal, and peanut butter. Water attracts it for drinking and bathing.

Winter
Breeding
All year

Scarlet Tanager   *Piranga olivacea*

Identification: The 7-inch, brilliant red scarlet tanager male has glossy black wings and tail and no crest. Females and immature birds—and males in winter—have dull green backs, yellow bellies, and blackish wings and tails.

Voice: Sounding like an American robin with a sore throat, the male scarlet tanager sings a series of 4 or 5 hoarse, caroling notes, *queer-it, queeer, queer-it, queer*. Its call is *chip-churr*.

Behavior: Male scarlet tanagers arrive at their breeding territory several days before the females. They sing from the tallest trees to attract females and defend their turf.

Habitat: In summer, thick groves of deciduous and coniferous trees, parks, and suburban backyards.

Natural food: Insects, berries and other fruits, and seeds. Scarlet tanagers forage both in the trees in which they sing and nest and on the ground beneath.

Nest: Well out on a limb, 8 to 75 feet above the ground, the female scarlet tanager builds a flat nest cup of twigs and rootlets lined with fine grasses. She then lays 3 to 5 pale blue or green eggs spotted with brown. She alone incubates the eggs, for 13 or 14 days, but both parents feed the young during the 2 weeks they remain in the nest.

How to attract: Tall deciduous trees help attract these birds. Scarlet tanagers will eat cornmeal mixed with peanut butter and suet. They will also bathe and drink water from backyard ponds.

Winter
Breeding
All year

Western Tanager   *Piranga ludoviciana*

Winter
Breeding
All year

Identification: With a beautiful red head and face, a yellow body, and black wings marked with 2 prominent white or yellowish bars, the 7-inch western tanager male is a striking bird. Males in winter, and females all year, are dull olive green above and yellow below, with wing bars.

Voice: The hoarse, robinlike song of the male is sung in 2 or 3 liquid phrases. Its call or alarm is *pit-trick.*

Behavior: These quiet birds of the high West spend much of their time in the tops of trees, often on the same perches for long periods of time. Though the birds blend into their habitat, making them difficult to see, you can locate singing males by searching in the direction of their songs.

Habitat: Coniferous and pine-oak forests.

Natural food: Mostly insects with berries and other fruits.

Nest: The western tanager's nest is usually saddled 20 to 30 feet above the ground in the fork of a horizontal branch in a pine, fir, oak, or aspen tree. The flat, loosely built cup of coniferous twigs and rootlets is lined with hair and rootlets. The 3 to 5 spotted bluish green eggs are incubated by the female for 13 days. Both parents feed the young.

How to attract: Offer citrus fruit and its juice, also hummingbird feeders. During migration, these birds feed in western flowering eucalyptus; they may nest in tall pines.

Northern Cardinal   *Cardinalis cardinalis*

Winter
Breeding
All year

Identification: The spectacular 8-inch northern cardinal male is brilliant red with a patch of black at the base of its conical red bill and a prominent crest that it can raise or lower for effect. The attractive female is the same shape, but in yellow tan plumage accented with red wings, crest, tail, and bill.

Voice: The male's *what-cheer, what-cheer, birdie, birdie, birdie* song is a welcome sound at any time of the year. The female may call the same notes, but more softly. Their forceful alarm call is a harsh *chip.*

Behavior: Northern cardinals use their heavy, sharp bills to crack seeds.

Habitat: Thickets, forest edges, suburban hedges, and garden shrubbery.

Natural food: Seeds in winter; a variety of beetles, cicadas, and other insects during warm months; and the fruits of trees, shrubs, and vines when available.

Nest: The northern cardinal hides its bulky nest of twigs, vines, and leaves in a deep thicket, generally no higher than 10 feet above the ground. The female lines the nest with fine grasses and hair, sometimes assisted by the male. The 3 or 4 bluish or greenish white eggs blotched with brown spots are incubated by the female, and occasionally by the male, for 12 or 13 days. The young fly about 12 days after hatching.

How to attract: Northern cardinals are fond of sunflower seeds, cracked corn, and safflower seeds. They will also bathe and drink from garden ponds.

Rose-breasted Grosbeak *Pheucticus ludovicianus*

Identification: A heavy, conical bill and the male's rosy red bib give the 8-inch rose-breasted grosbeak its name. The male is strikingly patterned in black and white with a heart-shaped red bib and a cream-colored bill. His flashy flight pattern is highlighted by pink underwing linings. The female is dramatically duller, with brown and white stripes and a white line above the eye.

Voice: The male's song resembles that of the American robin, only richer and more melodious. The alarm note is a loud *chink*.

Behavior: Rose-breasted grosbeaks are quiet birds of summer that sing beautifully, appear to be devoted mates, and visit feeders throughout the breeding season.

Habitat: Mature deciduous woodland, swamp borders, and orchards, as well as backyards and gardens surrounded by mature woods.

Natural food: Tree blossoms, seeds, and insects in deciduous treetops.

Nest: The usual nesting site of a rose-breasted grosbeak is 10 to 15 feet above the ground in the fork of a deciduous tree or shrub. The flimsy nest of sticks isn't dense enough to mask the 4 pale green, brown-blotched eggs when viewed from the ground. Both parents incubate for 12 to 14 days, often singing as they sit on the nest. Young fly at about 15 days of age.

How to attract: Plant shrubs and trees that produce flowers and berries or other fruit. Offer sunflower seeds and a birdbath.

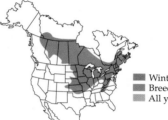

Winter
Breeding
All year

Black-headed Grosbeak *Pheucticus melanocephalus*

Identification: The 7-inch black-headed grosbeak male has a conical bill. Patterned in rich orange and black, it has a black head and black and white wings. The female is a warm brown with black and white head stripes.

Voice: The song of the black-headed grosbeak is a rich version of the American robin's, with more trilling notes and more abrupt phrases.

Behavior: Male black-headed grosbeaks arrive at their breeding grounds a week before females. When the females arrive, males begin their courtship, singing during hovering flight (otherwise, most singing is from a high perch).

Habitat: Second growth deciduous and coniferous forests, willow and cottonwood thickets, orchards, and western backyards and gardens where mature woodland prevails.

Natural food: Seeds and buds of pines and other trees, wild fruits, and berries; also the insects found in the trees where the birds live.

Nest: Placed 4 to 12 feet high in the fork of a small tree, the bulky nest of twigs, rootlets, and grass stems is built by the female black-headed grosbeak. The 3 or 4 pale green eggs, dotted with brown, are incubated 12 or 13 days by both parents. The young birds are out of the nest about 12 days after hatching.

How to attract: Besides relishing sunflower and other seeds, black-headed grosbeaks are fond of a variety of coniferous and deciduous trees and shrubs.

Winter
Breeding
All year

Indigo Bunting *Passerina cyanea*

Winter
Breeding
All year

Identification: In some light conditions, the plumage of the 5½-inch male indigo bunting looks black, but its usual appearance is deep indigo blue. The female looks so different in her plain brown plumage that she doesn't even appear to be of the same species.

Voice: The male's song of summer is a lazily unfolding rhythm—*sweet, sweet; zee, zee; seer, seer; sip, sip.* The alarm note is a simple *sick.*

Behavior: The male arrives on the breeding grounds in spring and defends its territory vigorously with singing late into the summer after most other birds have stopped their singing.

Habitat: Borders, edges, and brushy clearings where undergrowth is lush.

Natural food: Insects, berries, and seeds.

Nest: The crotch of a shrub or small tree, some 2 to 12 feet above the ground, is the usual site where the female indigo bunting carefully weaves her nest of grasses, bark strips, and weeds. She lines the nest with fine grasses and rootlets, and she alone incubates the 3 or 4 pale bluish white eggs for 12 or 13 days. In another 10 days the young leave.

How to attract: These avid seed eaters will come for thistle (niger), cracked sunflower seed, or millet during the summer breeding season, and they love birdbaths. Weedy edges of wooded gardens and annual and perennial seeds also attract them.

Painted Bunting *Passerina ciris*

Winter
Breeding
All year

Identification: Among the most beautifully colored of birds, the painted bunting male has a violet blue head, red underparts and rump, and a green back. The female of this 5¼-inch species is a very plain green above and lemon below.

Voice: From a high, visible perch, the male painted bunting sings its bright and pleasant warbling song. The alarm note of the species is a single sharp *chip.*

Behavior: Despite its gaudy appearance, the male painted bunting blends amazingly well in the lush vegetation in which it lives. The bird defends its territory with surprising aggression for a bird its size.

Habitat: Brushy fields, roadside hedges, fencerows, and thickets in southern backyards and gardens.

Natural food: Seeds and insects, foraged for on the ground.

Nest: The female painted bunting attaches her shallow nest cup to supporting vegetation 3 to 6 feet above the ground in a small tree or shrub. The 3 or 4 pale white eggs spotted with reddish brown are incubated by the female alone for 11 or 12 days. When young leave the nest at 2 weeks of age, the female continues to feed them while gathering nesting material for her next brood.

How to attract: Though many painted buntings leave the country during the winter months, many others remain and are faithful visitors to gardens in the Southeast where they find seeds to eat and pools for bathing and drinking.

Rufous-sided Towhee   *Pipilo erythrophthalmus*

Identification: Slightly smaller and more slender than an American robin, the 8-inch rufous-sided towhee male is mostly black with a white belly and reddish flanks. White on its wings and outer tail feathers flashes in flight. The female is brown where the male is black. In most regions, both sexes have red eyes.

Voice: The familiar spring song of the male rufous-sided towhee is *drink your teeeee*. The alarm call of the species is *che-wink*. (In the West, the song is a long, ringing *cheeee*, the alarm call a whining, descending *neyyyea*.)

Behavior: If you hear something thrashing around in dead leaves under a shrub, it could be a rufous-sided towhee searching for food.

Habitat: Thickets, hedgerows, fencerows, chaparral, brushy woodland, and the shrubbery of backyards and gardens.

Natural food: Insects, spiders, snails, and other organisms found under the dead leaves of a thicket; also berries and other fruits found on or near the ground.

Nest: The female rufous-sided towhee spends about 5 days building her bulky leaf and twig nest, on or near the ground. After lining it with fine grasses and hair, she will lay 3 to 5 cream-colored eggs with reddish spots and incubate them for 12 or 13 days. The young remain in the nest for 10 to 12 days.

How to attract: Towhees will eat birdseed and suet from a tray feeder. They are also attracted to ponds, tangles, and thickets near woods.

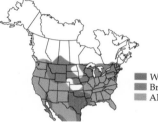

Winter
Breeding
All year

American Tree Sparrow   *Spizella arborea*

Identification: If it's summer, the little sparrow on the ground with a brick red cap is likely to be a chipping sparrow (page 54). In winter within its range, it is more likely to be the 6-inch American tree sparrow. Marked with a black dot in the center of its breast (unlike the chipping sparrow) and a bill that is dark above and light below, both male and female look alike.

Voice: Males tune up their cheerful, trilling song in spring before heading to their breeding grounds in the far North. Otherwise, a simple *teesip* note is uttered by the species.

Behavior: Misnamed "tree" sparrow because it looks like the tree sparrow of Europe, the American tree sparrow actually spends most of its time on the ground.

Habitat: In winter, this species migrates south to the eastern United States and southern Canada, where it lives in brushy fields, in fencerows, and around backyard feeders.

Natural food: In winter, the seeds of weeds, grasses, and crops; in summer, also insects and berries.

Nest: The female builds a nest of grass and moss on or near the ground, then lays 3 to 5 pale greenish white eggs with brown speckles. She incubates them for 12 or 13 days, and the young leave the nest about 10 days after hatching, before they can fly.

How to attract: Offer birdseed mixtures with red and white millet. The American tree sparrow likes weedy garden edges and seeds of annuals and perennials.

Winter
Breeding
All year

Chipping Sparrow *Spizella passerina*

Winter
Breeding
All year

Identification: The 5-inch sparrow with brick red cap, warm brown back, and light underside that feeds on the ground in your garden is most likely a chipping sparrow. Check for a white line above a black line that runs through the eye. Juveniles have streaky brown caps and striped underparts (in winter all birds resemble immature birds without breast streaking). The two sexes look alike.

Voice: Its song is an insectlike trill. Its alarm call is a simple *tsip*.

Behavior: This common ground sparrow is tame and quiet, at home even at the back door.

Habitat: On the ground in and around towns, villages, farms, and pine plantations.

Natural food: Mostly grass and weed seeds, but also many insects during summer months.

Nest: The female builds her nest of fine grasses and weed stalks 3 to 10 feet above the ground, usually in a small conifer; she lines it with fine grasses and hair, sometimes human hair. The 4 bluish green eggs with dark blotches are incubated by the female for 11 to 14 days while her mate feeds her on the nest. The young fly at about 1½ weeks of age.

How to attract: Offer red and white millet and cracked corn, also water. Weedy garden edges are attractive, as are small seeds of annuals and perennials.

Song Sparrow *Melospiza melodia*

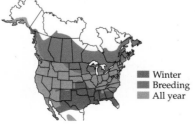

Winter
Breeding
All year

Identification: Most widespread of all North American sparrows, the 6-inch song sparrow has a brown back and a heavily streaked breast with a large central breast spot. Male and female look alike. The 30 or so recognized subspecies vary in coloration.

Voice: The song sparrow's song on the first warm day of spring is a most welcome sound. It begins with two ringing notes, *sweet, sweet*, and then launches into a jumble of various tones. The song sparrow's call or alarm note is a loud *chimp*.

Behavior: Tail dipping is common among song sparrows, but subspecies vary in other behavior and in voice.

Habitat: On or near the ground where there is an abundance of natural cover, on farms and in cities and suburbs.

Natural food: Insect matter foraged from the ground; also a variety of seeds, berries, and other fruits.

Nest: The well-hidden ground nest of the song sparrow is built by the female in 5 to 10 days, using grasses, weed stems, and leaves and a lining of fine grasses, rootlets, and hair. The 3 to 5 greenish white eggs, heavily dotted reddish brown, are incubated by the female for 12 or 13 days. The youngsters are out of the nest, often before they can fly, in about 10 days.

How to attract: Offer birdseed at ground feeders, and water. Also attractive are thickets, brush piles, and tangles (especially moist berry-producing plants).

White-throated Sparrow *Zonotrichia albicollis*

Identification: As its name indicates, the 6-inch white-throated sparrow has a white throat, but it also has a white-and-black-striped crown, a yellow patch in front of its eye, a streaked brown back, and a gray breast. Male and female look the same. Immature birds have tan-and-brown-striped crowns.

Voice: The white-throated sparrow's familiar song—*old sam peabody, peabody, peabody*—can be heard from late winter into spring. The call note of the species is a forceful *chink*.

Behavior: A scratcher, the gregarious white-throated sparrow is usually found or heard in thickets as it scratches up snow or dead leaves in search of food.

Habitat: Undergrowth and edges of fields and forests in the East, and eastern backyards and gardens during migrations.

Natural food: Weed seeds and the fruits of trees and shrubs, for which it forages on the ground in thickets; insects and other animal matter when available.

Nest: White-throated sparrows nest on or close to the ground under brush piles or fallen trees. The female builds a grass nest and lines it with pine needles and bark fibers for the 3 to 5 cream-colored eggs, heavily dotted with brown. She incubates the eggs for 12 to 14 days. Young leave the nest at about 10 days and learn to fly a few days later.

How to attract: In the East, offer red and white millet and cracked corn on or near the ground to attract white-throated sparrows during migrations.

Winter
Breeding
All year

White-crowned Sparrow *Zonotrichia leucophrys*

Identification: The rather large (6½-inch) white-crowned sparrow has a high, puffy white-and-black-striped crown, pale throat, gray breast, and brown streaked back. Its pink or yellow bill is another identifying mark. Both sexes look alike; young birds have tan-and-brown-striped crowns.

Voice: The first two notes of the white-crowned's song are sad whistles, followed by a jumbled trill. Its call or alarm is a smart *seet*.

Behavior: In winter, when they are most often seen, these birds live in flocks of 6 to 15 in the East and as many as 200 in the West.

Habitat: Alpine meadows, forest edges, clearings, brushy burns, chaparral, weedy fields, and backyards.

Natural food: Seeds, sprouts, and other plant material, as well as insects, on their principal subarctic breeding grounds (some subspecies nest in United States mountain ranges and along the West Coast). This bird is found scratching vigorously for food under leaves or snow.

Nest: Set into a matting of dense vegetation on or near the ground, the nest of the white-crowned sparrow is built by the female of fine twigs, grasses, and feathers and then lined with hair and feathers. The female incubates the 4 or 5 eggs, pale greenish with numerous reddish spots, for about 12 days. The young are out of the nest in another 10 days.

How to attract: During migrations, white-crowned sparrows will stop for birdseed on or near the ground. They relish weed seeds in any habitat.

Winter
Breeding
All year

Dark-eyed Junco *Junco hyemalis*

Winter
Breeding
All year

Identification: Sometimes called the "snowbird," the 6-inch dark-eyed junco is slate gray with a white belly and white outer tail feathers. The western form has a black head and brown back and wings. Male and female are similar, but immature birds are lighter in color.

Voice: The dark-eyed junco's musical spring trill is monotonous. Its winter call, *tic,* is heard often.

Behavior: Dark-eyed juncos forage for seeds on the ground in open areas. They're gregarious in winter, usually living in loose-knit flocks.

Habitat: Thickets and edges of coniferous woodland, mixed forests, and, in winter, backyards and gardens across the continent.

Natural food: Seeds, buds, and sprouts; in summer, insects found in coniferous forests.

Nest: Under an overhang of tree roots or a road embankment, the dark-eyed junco conceals its nest of grasses, rootlets, and mosses lined with finer plant materials and hair. The male helps carry materials for the female nest builder; she incubates her 4 or 5 pale gray eggs, marked with heavy reddish dots, for 12 or 13 days. Young leave the nest at about 2 weeks of age.

How to attract: Offer red and white millet, cracked corn, and other small grains on or near the ground. Conifers are attractive, as are weedy edges and seeds of annuals and perennials.

Red-winged Blackbird *Agelaius phoeniceus*

Winter
Breeding
All year

Identification: This 9-inch black bird with a red and yellow chevron on each wing is one of the most widespread and best-known birds on the continent. Females are quite different in their sparrowlike brown-striped plumage. Young birds resemble females.

Voice: The *kong-ga-ree* song of the male redwing heralds spring from still-frozen marshes across the North. The birds' *chink* call or alarm note sounds quite demanding.

Behavior: Male redwings arrive at their breeding grounds before the females, set up territories, and defend them vigorously against other males. If there is a surplus of females, males may be polygamous.

Habitat: Fresh and saltwater marshes; swamps; wet meadows, pastures, and roadside ditches.

Natural food: Three-quarters vegetable matter (cultivated grains, weed seeds, and fruits), the rest animal matter (insects, spiders, mollusks, and snails).

Nest: In loose colonies, female redwings build nests amidst cattails, reeds, grasses, cultivated crops, and shrubs, usually near water. The nests are constructed of grasses, sedge leaves, and rushes bound to living vegetation and lined with fine grasses. The 3 or 4 pale blue eggs, scrawled in brown and purple, are incubated by the female for 10 to 12 days. The young climb out of the nest in about 10 days and then learn to fly.

How to attract: Cracked corn offered in any kind of bird feeder, but preferably a tray, will attract red-winged blackbirds, even while they are nesting nearby.

Meadowlark (Eastern & Western) *Sturnella magna, Sturnella neglecta*

Identification: Though separate species, the two meadowlarks are virtually identical in appearance (a western is shown at right). Chunky 10-inch birds with short tails, long bills, and buff brown backs, both are distinguished by a dramatic black V falling from the throat onto the yellow breast. Male and female are equally colorful.

Voice: Only by their songs can one easily differentiate between the two meadowlarks. The western's song is melodious, with a flutelike babbling and gurgling; the eastern's is a more homogeneous, plaintive whistling. The western's call is a sharp *chuck*, the eastern's a buzzing *dzrrt*.

Behavior: The males of both species sing from fence posts or utility wires within their nesting territories; they may be polygamous. Females are very secretive.

Habitat: Open grassy fields, meadows, and prairies.

Natural food: Insects (three-quarters of their diet) and grain. The birds forage by walking, not hopping.

Nest: The nests of both species are located in ground depressions in grassy fields. The female alone builds the nest in about a week's time, using dried grass and topping the structure with a domed roof. The 3 to 5 spotted white eggs are incubated by the female for 13 to 15 days; both sexes bring food to the young, who leave the nest in about 2 weeks.

How to attract: Backyards with prairielike conditions—large, unmowed lawns and fields of short grass—may attract meadowlarks searching for nesting sites and grain.

Western   Eastern

Common Grackle *Quiscalus quiscula*

Identification: A 12-inch-long glossy black bird with a purple, bronze, and greenish cast, the common grackle has a long, keel-shaped tail, a long bill, and yellow eyes. The female is less glossy than the male.

Voice: The male's song is a rasping *chu-seek* that sounds like a rusty gate swinging on its hinges; it is uttered when the bird ruffles its feathers in display for a female. Its call is a shrill *chuck*.

Behavior: During winter and migration, common grackles gather with European starlings, red-winged blackbirds, and brown-headed cowbirds in huge flocks that roost together—and sometimes disturb people living nearby.

Habitat: Cities, suburbs, farmland, pine plantations, and marshes.

Natural food: Insects, earthworms, salamanders, mice, the eggs and young of smaller birds, and the nuts and seeds of trees, shrubs, and crops.

Nest: Most often in colonies of 20 to 30 pairs, common grackles nest as much as 60 feet above the ground in trees, usually coniferous. The female builds a bulky nest of grasses, debris, and sometimes mud, then lines it with grasses, feathers, and debris; the task takes her about 11 days to complete. The 5 pale greenish white eggs, scrawled with brown and purple, are incubated by the female for 11 or 12 days. Young can fly at about 2 weeks.

How to attract: Though unpopular with some people, common grackles will come for birdseed (particularly cracked corn) and suet in spring and fall.

Winter
Breeding
All year

Brown-headed Cowbird   *Molothrus ater*

Winter
Breeding
All year

Identification: The 7-inch male brown-headed cowbird has a chocolate brown head, a glossy black body, and a conical bill. The female looks completely different, with mouse gray plumage and a lighter throat. Immature birds are paler than females and have heavily streaked underparts.

Voice: The male's song is a series of high-pitched, watery, bubbly notes. The call note is *chuck.*

Behavior: In spring, a female cowbird attracts an entourage of 3 to 5 male suitors, all displaying for her and attempting to mate with her before she selects the host nests into which she will lay her eggs (see "Nest," at right).

Habitat: Farmland, forest edges, swamps, open fields, and suburban backyards.

Natural food: A combination of insects, grains, and berries.

Nest: Cowbirds build no nests. Instead, the female distributes as many as 20 grayish white eggs marked with brown dots in the nests of other birds. She removes an egg from each "host" bird's nest and replaces it with her own. The host then raises the nestling cowbird—sometimes at the expense of its own young, which may be pushed out, smothered, or starved by competition from the larger cowbird chick. The foster parents rear the alien youngster until it can procure its own food.

How to attract: Cowbirds often show up with other blackbirds and will eat cracked corn and millet.

Northern Oriole   *Icterus galbula*

Winter
Breeding
All year

Identification: The brilliant orange and black male of the eastern race of the northern oriole (the Baltimore oriole) has a jet black head. But the western male has a black crown, orange cheeks, and an orange line above the eye. Females have olive brown backs and are burnt orange (eastern) or gray (western) below. These birds are 7½ to 8½ inches long.

Voice: The song is a series of disjointed, flutelike whistles. The call is a two-part, chattering *hue-lee.*

Behavior: Male northern orioles arrive at their nesting sites a few days before the females to begin singing and defending their territories against other orioles.

Habitat: Orchards and shade trees.

Natural food: Insects found in the trees where they live; also the tree fruit, including cherries and citrus.

Nest: Northern orioles build hanging basketlike nests 6 to 60 feet above the ground in elms, willows, and apple trees. The female spends 4 to 8 days weaving a deep pouch attached by its rim to drooping branches; the nest is lined with hair, wool, and fine grasses. The 4 pale greenish eggs, scrawled with brown, are incubated by the female for 12 to 14 days. In another 2 weeks, the young are on the wing.

How to attract: Northern orioles will sip the juices from orange or grapefruit halves. They also drink sugar water from hummingbird feeders and splash and drink at birdbaths. They nest in tall poplars, willows, and cottonwoods.

Purple Finch *Carpodacus purpureus*

Identification: Raspberry is closer than purple to the true color of the 6-inch male purple finch. Most of the coloration is concentrated around the head, upper parts, and breast; the belly and undertail coverts are white. Females and young birds resemble large, heavily striped brown sparrows. Both sexes have deeply notched tails.

Voice: The fast and lively warble of the male purple finch usually repeats each note in the series. The call or alarm note is a quick *pik*.

Behavior: Purple finches spend the winter in large flocks, wandering farther south in years when food is scarce in their coniferous forest breeding grounds.

Habitat: Coniferous forests, pine plantations, and suburban backyards where evergreens are prominent.

Natural food: The seeds of trees and shrubs in winter; also some insects from the coniferous forests in which it lives.

Nest: Invariably, the female purple finch builds her nest 5 to 60 feet above the ground on the horizontal limb of a conifer. The neatly built cup of twigs, grasses, and weed stems is lined with fine grasses and hair. The female alone incubates the 3 to 5 greenish spotted eggs for 13 days. The young leave in about 2 weeks.

How to attract: Sunflower seeds, in the shell and cracked, are a favorite food. Purple finches are lured by moving water, also berries, fruits, and buds of deciduous trees. Conifers attract them for nesting.

Winter
Breeding
All year

House Finch *Carpodacus mexicanus*

Identification: More heavily striped than the purple finch, the 6-inch male house finch has a brownish cap but otherwise is orange red on the head, bib, and rump. Females and immature birds are heavily streaked with brown and have less of a facial pattern than their purple finch counterparts. The tails of both sexes are brown and squared.

Voice: The lively warbling song of both the male and female house finch is uttered in phrases of three notes. The call or alarm is a *sweet queet*.

Behavior: Once restricted to the Southwest, the adaptable house finch is thriving in the East after being released on Long Island in the 1920s.

Habitat: A great variety of habitats, from desert to open forests, farmland to towns.

Natural food: Seeds of trees, shrubs, and crops. The house finch is also fond of cultivated fruits and has been known to cause damage in orchards.

Nest: The female house finch carefully builds a cup of twigs 5 to 7 feet above the ground in a natural cavity, mailbox, building, birdhouse, or vine. The 4 or 5 sparsely dotted, pale bluish green eggs are incubated by the female for 13 days while she is fed by the male, who regurgitates food to her. Young leave the nest in 2 to 3 weeks.

How to attract: House finches are frequent patrons of feeders that offer sunflower and thistle seeds—or birdseed mix. They consume a variety of seeds and berries from garden plants, also unopened buds of fruit trees.

Winter
Breeding
All year

Pine Siskin   *Carduelis pinus*

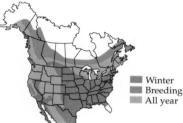

Winter
Breeding
All year

Identification: The small, brown, heavily streaked 5-inch pine siskin has bright yellow in the wings and at the base of the tail. Male and female look alike.

Voice: The pine siskin's song is a somewhat insectlike, buzzing trill that rises in pitch. Its call or alarm note is *tsee-ee.*

Behavior: A shortage of tree seeds in the northern forests will send the siskins southward to search for food. Highly gregarious, they travel in flocks of more than 100 birds, sometimes swirling into treetops like blown leaves.

Habitat: Northern coniferous forests; also near backyard feeders.

Natural food: Seeds from pines, spruces, firs, and other trees and shrubs; also insects, tree sap, and the nectar of tree blossoms found in their coniferous forest habitat.

Nest: Often nesting in loose colonies, female pine siskins conceal their nests of twigs, mosses, and lichens 6 to 35 feet above the ground on horizontal branches of conifers. Mosses, rootlets, hair, fur, and feathers are used to line the nests. The female lays one pale greenish blue egg a day for 3 or 4 days, beginning incubation with the first egg to reduce the risk of freezing. The young hatch on consecutive days after 13 days of incubation. The female incubates alone while the male feeds her on the nest. The young fly in about 2 weeks.

How to attract: Put out thistle seeds and cracked sunflower seeds—and watch for flocks of 50 to 200. Water, the catkins of alders, and the conelike fruit of birches also appeal to pine siskins.

American Goldfinch   *Carduelis tristis*

Winter
Breeding
All year

Identification: In summer, the 5-inch American goldfinch male is bright canary yellow with white wing bars and a black cap, wings, and tail. The female is olive yellow with brownish black wings and tail and white wing bars. In winter, both sexes look like the summer female, but browner.

Voice: The sweet song of the male American goldfinch is canarylike, rising and falling. The *per-chick-a-ree* flight call is uttered with each undulation. The call is *see-me.*

Behavior: Gregarious most of the year, these "wild canaries" live in loose flocks of several pairs in summer, dozens and even hundreds of birds in winter.

Habitat: Open fields, farmland, fencerows, groves, villages, and suburban backyards.

Natural food: Seeds of thistles, dandelions, goldenrods, weeds, vegetables, and trees throughout the year, and insects when available.

Nest: Nesting in late summer to coincide with maturing thistles, the female goldfinch builds a tight, dense cup of vegetable fibers lined with thistledown and cattail down, choosing a site 4 to 14 feet above the ground in an upright fork of a tree. The male feeds the female through the 12- to 14-day incubation of their 4 to 6 pale bluish white eggs. Both parents feed their offspring regurgitated, partially digested seeds during the 2 weeks the youngsters are in the nest.

How to attract: Offering water and thistle and/or sunflower seeds is likely to attract goldfinches throughout the year.

Evening Grosbeak   *Coccothraustes vespertinus*

Identification: The chunky, 8-inch evening grosbeak male has a large, conical bill, pale in color. Yellow brown with a darker head, he has a short black tail and black and white wings. The female is silvery cream with black and cream wings. Both sexes look flashy in flight due to their white secondary flight feathers.

Voice: Noisy birds, the evening grosbeaks *chip* and *chirp* and *clee-ip* constantly. The male's song is a lively but disjointed warble.

Behavior: In the wintertime, evening grosbeaks are gregarious birds that will fly southward in large flocks to search for food if the seeds of coniferous trees are scarce in the North.

Habitat: Northern coniferous forests and mixed woodland.

Natural food: Primarily seeds and buds of both coniferous and deciduous trees, as well as berries and other fruits; also insects associated with their habitat.

Nest: The female evening grosbeak builds a fragile nest of twigs and mosses, lined with rootlets, some 20 to 60 feet above the ground in a conifer. The 3 or 4 clear blue eggs, blotched with brown and purple, are incubated by the female for 12 to 14 days. The young remain in the nest for about 2 weeks.

How to attract: Sunflower seeds in the shell are very popular and may be consumed in great quantity at stationary feeders with trays or sturdy perches. These birds also like to bathe and drink at ponds and to eat the winged pods of such deciduous trees as maple and box elder.

■ Winter
■ Breeding
■ All year

House Sparrow   *Passer domesticus*

Identification: In its breeding plumage, the 6-inch male house sparrow has a gray top, chestnut nape, black bib, brown back, and gray belly. Females and young birds lack the black bib, and males in winter have less black.

Voice: A noisy, chattering bird, the house sparrow twitters and chips most of the time but has no real song.

Behavior: Really a weaver and not a sparrow, this species was introduced into North America more than a century ago. Since then it has spread throughout the continent. House sparrows are found in many other parts of the world as well.

Habitat: Cities, villages, suburbs, and farms.

Natural food: Mostly vegetable matter, despite the fact that house sparrows were once thought to control destructive insects. They thrived when horses were the primary mode of transportation, ensuring an abundance of grain and seed from straw.

Nest: As is typical of weavers, a pair of house sparrows builds its huge ball nest of grass, weeds, and trash, open on one side, inside a cavity or birdhouse, on a rafter, or behind loose boards or shutters on a building. The 5 heavily spotted white eggs are incubated by the female for 12 or 13 days, and the young leave when they are 15 to 17 days old.

How to attract: The house sparrow will soon find you, especially if you offer cracked corn, red and white millet, and other seeds.

■ Winter
■ Breeding
■ All year

As natural to gardens as flowers and foliage, birds add music, color, and graceful motion. Pausing on this sheltered branch is a Carolina chickadee (see page 38).

Birdscaping Your Yard

*I*f your garden is "squeaky clean,"
it's not a paradise for birds. The impeccably manicured landscape—
constantly raked, mowed, pruned, and sprayed for pests—usually
offers little to attract birds, even less to hold their interest. The garden
that approximates a wild, natural environment is far more likely to
catch a bird's attention.

But don't assume that cutting back on maintenance must result
in an untidy-looking garden. All you have to do is let nature take
the lead. Choose plants that will attract birds, and arrange them to
suit birds' needs. Then let the plants grow and mingle with as little
restrictive pruning as possible. Keep in mind the ultimate sizes of
plants when you lay out your garden, and you will be able to respect
their natural growth habits as the garden develops.

Any bird's needs are simple, if not always easily met: food, shelter (including nesting habitat), and water. A thoughtfully planned
garden can provide it all. No single landscape will satisfy all needs
for all the species of birds that may visit it—but you certainly will
be able to give birds a sense of welcome and to encourage greater
numbers and varieties of them to stop by. In this chapter, you'll read
about the basics of "birdscaping" a backyard habitat and learn which
plants are good choices for attracting birds to your own garden.

Creating a Habitat for Birds

How can you turn your garden into a bird sanctuary or habitat? The answer depends on your garden's location and the needs of local birds that you hope to attract. Bird species support themselves in almost every imaginable habitat, natural or man-made. Still, to attract as great a number and diversity as possible, plan to provide what birds of your locality need.

Consider both residents and temporary visitors, and start by understanding the four essential resources that a habitat provides—food, water, shelter, and a place to raise young. If you also plan to compensate for any scarcity in your area, you'll greatly boost your yard's attractiveness to birds. In the desert, water is often scarce; where winters are extremely cold and barren, food and shelter are critically needed.

Food. What birds eat from a garden habitat is a broad spectrum of foods. Directly from plants come such fleshy fruits as cherries, holly berries, and cane fruits like blackberry and raspberry. Nuts—acorns, for example—are favored by some species, while a vast array of birds seek out seeds of grasses, annuals, perennials, and some shrubs and trees. A smorgasbord of insects and other invertebrates—from earthworms and caterpillars to flies, aphids, and microscopic mites—provides important dietary protein to some species. Some birds consume insects year-round, while virtually all garden birds forage for them during the demanding breeding season when there are nestlings to feed. Hawks and owls eat small animals, such as mice.

Don't forget water. All birds need water, just as they need food. Water for drinking is a daily necessity, but almost equally important is the availability of shallow water for bathing. If you provide a water source designed for birds and situated within quick reach of cover, you will have a powerful garden attraction for a wide assortment of feathered friends. Keep the water clean, and make sure it doesn't freeze in winter. Guidelines for planning a bird's pool or birdbath are given on page 72.

Shelter and cover. Birds rely on plants to provide shelter from the elements as well as cover from predators. Shelter may mean relief from midday sun or a place to roost for the night—or it may mean refuge from soaking rain, biting wind, or freezing cold. Almost anything leafy will serve for shade or an overnight stay, but it takes a heavier canopy of foliage to shield against harsher elements. Where winter lows drop to zero or below, needle-leafed evergreen trees and shrubs are a must for birds that stay in the area. Even in milder climates, birds appreciate groups of dense, broad-leafed evergreen trees, shrubs, and vines for shelter from rain and wind.

Birds seek different kinds of cover depending on which predators they're evading. Potential hawk prey often find enough protection on a convenient tree limb. Thick shrubbery provides a good hideaway from a feline hunter, as long as it's open enough for a quick entry by the bird yet dense enough to foil or slow down the cat. (Be sure to plant shrubs far enough away that they don't become the cat's cover for a sneak attack on the birdbath or feeder.)

Thorns offer an asset to any foliaged hideaway for birds, since they deter predators. Even better than a single shrub is a grouping that approximates a natural thicket or tangle.

Nesting sites. Birds use as many different styles of housing as do humans. Some nest on the ground in grasses or under foliage. Some nest in shrubbery at varying heights. Others prefer "high-rise" accommodations, seeking out structural sites that range from cavities in tree trunks to convenient nooks and ledges on buildings.

Some birds live and breed comfortably in urban and suburban environments, while others nest in remote areas, visiting a residential garden only for food or water—or during migration. At nesting time, some birds occupy a large territory, each pair keeping away others of its kind (though not necessarily other species).

This East Coast garden offers many inducements for birds in early autumn. From left, cedar waxwings dine on dogwood berries; more berries grow on evergreen holly, and tree sparrow perches on seed-laden Pennisetum. Fading gloriosa daisy attracts pine siskin as purple finches dip in birdbath. Evening grosbeaks snack at sunflower seed feeder hung from red oak tree, and downy woodpecker clings to suet feeder. Viburnum below tree and Euonymus alata in background yield more food; blue spruce branches offer refuge if needed.

. . . Creating a Habitat for Birds

A richly varied birdscape

Variety is not only the spice of life, but also the key to planting a widely appealing birdscape. The landscaping trend toward design simplicity based on repeated use of just a few different plants will produce a habitat of limited practical value to birds. Instead, aim for a smorgasbord effect.

In nature, birds are accustomed to the mingling of diverse plants. The greatest mixture of bird species occurs in nature where different assortments of plants meet in what savvy bird gardeners call "edges" or "ecotones." In a garden birdscape, this means an arrangement of plants similar to what occurs where a woodland makes a transition to meadow or grassland. Primary forest trees gradually give way to shorter forest-edge, understory trees, which in turn merge with lower shrubbery that rambles into a grassy clearing.

This "edge," whether natural or created, includes habitats for a number of different birds—those that prefer high tree canopies, those that seek middle and lower levels, and those that feed low in grasses or on the ground. Some birds flutter at all levels, singing at one height, nesting at another, and feeding elsewhere.

In contrast to a naturalistic "edge" effect, a broad, carefully manicured lawn is usually the least attractive garden feature for birds. There are a few exceptions, such as the robins that hop across after a rain shower in search of earthworms; but to most birds, the expanse of closely cropped lawn represents vulnerability to predators without nearby cover to which they can quickly fly. In nature, a grassy field at least offers a seasonal banquet of seeds, as well as shaggy concealment—bonuses lost to a well-groomed lawn.

For a more abundantly welcoming birdscape, let the following points guide your garden planning. Then you can fill out your plan by selecting specific plants.

■ Plant some or all of the birdscape's border with varied trees and shrubs (or begin the garden where trees and shrubs are already established). Let large shade trees provide the canopy, while shorter trees create an understory. Have shrubbery emerge from the trees to form a bridge into open space. In a small garden, it works just as well to borrow from adjacent gardens by letting neighboring trees serve as the canopy.

■ Limit lawns to small areas, placing mass plantings of graduated trees and shrubs around lawn perimeters. Shrubs that directly border the lawn should branch low to the ground. If your garden presently includes vast expanses of lawn, consider breaking up the turf by planting islands or groups of trees with shrubs at their bases.

■ In cold-winter regions, if space permits, it helps to include a stand of dense evergreen trees for winter shelter. Ideally, these should grow at the northern edge of the garden so as not to block winter sun. But if trees won't suit your birdscaping plans, consider a hedge of hemlock (*Tsuga*) to serve the same sheltering purpose.

■ Allow a "wild area" if you can spare a garden corner just for the use of birds. Let grasses grow high to produce seeds, as well as a congenial dining area for ground-feeding birds. Let a thorny, dense shrub (such as *Rosa multiflora*) grow into a tangled thicket for nesting and refuge. Also good at tangling are various brambles (*Rubus*)—or let vines scramble through and over massed shrubbery. If a tree dies or drops a limb, let the wood decay naturally; birds will savor its insects and may use it for nesting.

■ Include a garden oasis, however small, where water will be available to birds for drinking and bathing (see page 72 for pointers and pages 106–108 for pools and birdbaths to build yourself). Birds also benefit from dust baths, which help them cleanse their feathers of parasites, so leave a few patches of bare earth in protected places.

Planning, then planting

Whether you are starting from scratch or remodeling an existing yard, your project will be easier to carry out if you sketch your property on graph paper that will give you a scaled-down model of exact dimensions.

Draw in the outline of your house, as well as outdoor structures such as patio, walks, and fencing. Mark locations of existing plants you want to keep. Note the property's physical character, such as sloping or shady areas or changes in soil quality. All these factors are likely to influence your plant selection.

As you choose plants, use the descriptions that start on page 68, plus the more specific list for

your region given on pages 81–83, for guidance. Visit a good local nursery, arboretum, or botanic garden to view plants and to see which species and varieties are especially good for your area.

Plants that are native to your locality are generally both easiest to care for and attractive to resident birds. A garden that goes through seasonal changes is also likely to appeal more both to you and to birds. It offers variety through the year in flowers, fruit, and foliage, while also giving birds a spectrum of foods and habitat conditions.

If your climate is cold in winter, be sure to include plants that can provide food and shelter to birds who winter in the area. Some fruits of summer and autumn are greedily consumed as soon as ripe, but others are passed over initially in favor of tastier choices. Later, in winter and early spring, such plants as *Berberis* (barberry), *Cotoneaster*, *Crataegus* (hawthorn), *Ilex* (holly), *Juniperus* (juniper), *Lonicera* (honeysuckle), *Mahonia*, *Myrica* (bayberry), and *Sorbus* (mountain ash) offer nourishment when it is most needed.

Insects interest them, too

Though gardeners may see insects as adversaries, many birds know them as food. Some birds, called insectivores, dine almost exclusively on insect life, busily exploring every nook and cranny for beetles, worms, flies, mosquitoes, and more—even the eggs of insects. When nestlings need food, the interest in protein-rich insects rises sharply.

You can't depend on birds to eliminate all harmful insects from your garden—but birds may keep them at a tolerable level for the health and appearance of your plants. Occasionally you may need to combat an exploded population of a damaging insect (mites or scale, for example). Under such circumstances, always choose the least toxic spray option, follow directions to the letter, and spray only infested plants (also see page 91).

Some trees and shrubs routinely attract insects that will lure birds. Among trees are *Acer* (maple), *Alnus* (alder), *Betula* (birch), *Cornus* (dogwood), *Crataegus* (hawthorn), *Quercus* (oak), and *Rhamnus* (buckthorn). Insect-populated shrubs include *Arctostaphylos* (manzanita), *Cornus* (dogwood), *Lonicera* (honeysuckle), and *Rhamnus* (buckthorn).

Eliminating pesticides from your garden will increase its wholesome appeal to birds.

A Safe Route

The garden shown in the plan below hosts more than two dozen kinds of birds by virtue of its thoughtful landscaping.

A protective trail was planted between the neighbor's willow tree (upper left) and the feeders outside the kitchen window (lower right). Ground-feeding birds travel low along the route in dense shrubbery; pine siskins, chickadees, and kinglets approach the feeders via the sides and tops of trees. Bushtits and various warblers, simply work the plants themselves, ignoring the feeders.

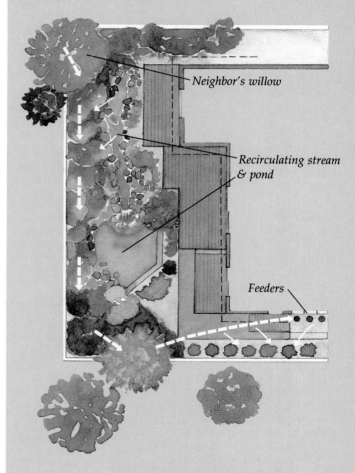

Neighbor's willow

Recirculating stream & pond

Feeders

Landscape architect: Steve Lindjord.

Trees

Cornus florida (flowering dogwood)

Birds rely on trees both for shelter (nest sites as well as protective cover) and for seeds, fruit, and insects. Here are some bird favorites. Check pages 81–83 for what grows best in your region. Hummingbird favorites are listed separately on page 79.

ABIES
FIR

Value to birds: Seeds, insects, shelter.
Used by: Chickadees, creepers, doves, finches, flycatchers, hawks, jays, juncos, kinglets, nuthatches, owls, robins, swallows, thrushes, towhees, vireos, warblers, waxwings, woodpeckers.

Evergreen. Thick canopies of foliage offer good shelter, especially welcome in snowy winter. Many birds relish seeds scattered when cones ripen in spring and summer. Tall, spirelike firs prefer a cool, moist atmosphere and clean air, are most successful in northern states and southward in mountainous areas.

ACER
MAPLE

Value to birds: Buds, seeds, shelter.
Used by: Finches, grosbeaks, orioles, robins, vireos, warblers, waxwings.

Deciduous. Nearly all have dense, sheltering foliage, and all bear seeds (ripening in late summer or early fall) in papery casings. There are maples for nearly all climates, a range of sizes and shapes. Virtually all exhibit fall foliage color in yellow, orange, or red tones. Most have extensive, shallow root systems that need regular moisture; because of root competition, the best plantings near maples will be vigorous shrubs, ground covers, or lawn.

ALNUS
ALDER

Value to birds: Seeds, pollen, shelter.
Used by: Finches, mourning doves, nuthatches, warblers, woodpeckers.

Deciduous. In winter, pendant seed catkins attract a number of birds. In the growing season, insects feed various songbirds; sapsuckers mine trunks. Fast-growing alders show kinship to birches in smooth trunks, foliage crowns usually taller than wide. Like birches, they grow best with regular moisture, are attractive in groves. Fall foliage color is yellow to rusty brown.

AMELANCHIER
SERVICEBERRY, SHADBLOW

Value to birds: Fruit.
Used by: Crows, grosbeaks, tanagers, thrushes, vireos, waxwings, woodpeckers.

Deciduous. Most serviceberries are shrubby, but three species—*A. arborea, A. canadensis,* and *A. laevis*—become graceful small- to medium-sized trees. Showy clusters of white or pinkish flowers appear in early spring before leaves emerge. By summer, small dark blue berries attract many birds. In autumn, foliage turns red or yellow. These are lightweight, forest-edge plants.

BETULA
BIRCH

Value to birds: Buds, seeds, insects.
Used by: Bushtits, chickadees, finches (including pine siskins), nuthatches, sapsuckers, towhees, woodpeckers.

Deciduous. Birds are lured by seed catkins that hang from bare winter branches. During growing season, plentiful insects attract more birds. Denizens of northern latitudes and high altitudes, some birches also adapt well to more temperate lowland gardens. All prefer regular moisture and have somewhat competitive roots near the surface. Fresh green foliage turns bright yellow in fall.

CARPINUS
HORNBEAM

Value to birds: Fruit, shelter.
Used by: Cardinals, goldfinches, grosbeaks.

Deciduous. In autumn, hanging clusters of nutlike fruits provide food. Pyramidal to round-headed, these medium-sized trees look neat all year. Dense, dark foliage turns brilliant yellow to red in fall.

CELTIS
HACKBERRY

Value to birds: Fruit, shelter.
Used by: Bluebirds, cardinals, grosbeaks, mockingbirds, orioles, pigeons, robins, thrushes, waxwings, woodpeckers.

Deciduous. Providing small clusters of berrylike fruits in fall, hackberries also offer the shade and grace of elms without the disease problem that makes elms risky. Deep-rooted, they won't crack pavement or compete with nearby plants. Most species leaf out late in spring, turning bright yellow in autumn.

CORNUS
DOGWOOD

Value to birds: Fruit, insects, shelter.
Used by: Bluebirds, cardinals, catbirds, finches, grosbeaks, mockingbirds, robins, tanagers, thrashers, thrushes, vireos, waxwings, woodpeckers.

Deciduous. Gardeners prize these trees for their spring flowers (actually showy bracts that surround tiny flowers); birds relish the fruits that follow. An insect population adds appeal. The shrub-tree *C. alternifolia* lacks showy floral display but provides plenty of fruit. Flowering dogwood (*C. florida*) is the most widely planted—a medium-sized tree with flowerlike bracts in white, pink, or nearly red. Larger trees, *C. controversa* and *C. nuttallii*, grow to 50 feet or more. All are attractive against taller evergreens. Autumn foliage may be yellow to red.

CRATAEGUS
HAWTHORN

Value to birds: Fruit, insects, shelter.
Used by: Grosbeaks, jays, mockingbirds, robins, waxwings.

Deciduous. These small to medium-sized trees offer colorful flowers, decorative fruits that are consumed by many birds, and colorful autumn foliage. Aphids are another lure to birds during the growing season. Most hawthorns are dense, armed with sharp thorns. Typically, white flowers appear after leaf-out in spring; clusters of red fruits (like tiny apples) ripen in summer or autumn. Named selections with double flowers generally produce no fruits.

ELAEAGNUS ANGUSTIFOLIA
RUSSIAN OLIVE

Value to birds: Fruit, shelter.
Used by: Cardinals, grosbeaks, jays, robins, waxwings.

Deciduous. After inconspicuous fragrant flowers of early summer comes a treat for birds—olivelike, silvery yellow fruits. Silvery gray foliage and graceful appearance mask a tough constitution. Fast-growing, this small tree thrives in poor, dry soil, summer heat, and winter cold.

ILEX
HOLLY

Value to birds: Fruit, shelter.
Used by: Cardinals, grosbeaks, jays, robins, waxwings.

Evergreen and deciduous. Dense, shiny, spiny evergreen leaves and fruits offer safe haven and delicious food to many birds. Several species develop into small to medium-sized trees. Most bear male and female flowers on separate plants; for female plants to produce berries, you need a male plant nearby (not necessarily of the same species). Provide good soil and regular moisture; hollies will thrive in partial shade, but berry production is better in full sun.

JUNIPERUS
JUNIPER

Value to birds: Fruit, shelter.
Used by: Cardinals, grosbeaks, phoebes, robins.

Evergreen. Some birds consume juniper berries, and many others welcome the evergreen winter shelter. Male and female flowers are usually borne on separate plants; to be sure a plant will bear fruit, buy when berries are present. Most available are lower-growing forms of species that are trees in the wild. Dense growth may contain two kinds of foliage: needlelike or spiny juvenile leaves and scalelike mature foliage. Foliage color may be green, steel blue, gray, or red-tinted in winter. All trees are strongly upright and fairly slow growing. They tolerate a variety of soils and drought.

LARIX
LARCH

Value to birds: Seeds, shelter.
Used by: Goldfinches, nuthatches, pine siskins.

Deciduous. Seed-laden cones provide fall and winter food to varied birds. Unlike related cone-bearing trees (such as firs and spruces), larches shed their needles in autumn and grow a fresh crop in spring. Small, seed-bearing cones resemble brown rose blossoms, creating polka-dot effect as they hang from bare limbs. In eastern regions, a small worm may attack immature foliage, ruining a tree's appearance for the season.

LIQUIDAMBAR STYRACIFLUA
AMERICAN SWEET GUM

Value to birds: Seeds, shelter.
Used by: Cardinals, chickadees, finches (including American goldfinches, house finches, pine siskins), juncos, robins.

Deciduous. Large, maplelike leaves assume broad range of fall colors. To birds, leaves offer shelter. Bare winter branches reveal seed-bearing fruits: spiny balls that hang from slender stalks. Mature specimens reach about 60 feet, only about half as wide. Grove plantings are especially attractive in gardens—and birds appreciate the abundance of food and protective shelter. In time, numerous surface roots may become intrusive, so plan carefully what you grow near American sweet gum.

MAGNOLIA
MAGNOLIA

Value to birds: Seeds, shelter.
Used by: Catbirds, mockingbirds, robins, thrushes, vireos.

Evergreen. Dense canopies of large leaves shelter birds, and conelike seed vessels provide them with food. Southern magnolia (*M. grandiflora*) grows to 80 feet, producing fragrant white flowers against polished, dark green leaves. Sweet bay (*M. virginiana*) features smaller, fragrant blossoms and smaller leaves of soft, grayish green on a large shrub or tree to 60 feet. Both magnolias need regular moisture; sweet bay will grow in nearly swampy soils.

MALUS
CRABAPPLE

Value to birds: Fruit, shelter.
Used by: Bluebirds, cedar waxwings, flycatchers, grosbeaks, mockingbirds, robins, thrushes, vireos.

Deciduous. Kin to apples, these 20- to 30-foot trees bear smaller fruits. Many species and named hybrids are sold. Spring flowers may be white, pink, or red, covering trees before leaf-out. Fruits range from yellow to red in color and from as small as cranberries to the size of small apples. Tart in flavor, fruits appeal strongly to a variety of birds.

The following crabapples will bear fruit regularly; those followed by (w) retain fruits late into the year, a special benefit to hungry birds: 'Adams', *M. atrosanguinea* (w), 'Blanche Ames', 'Dolgo', 'Dorothea', 'Flame', *M. floribunda*, 'Katherine' (w), 'Pink Spires', *M. purpurea* 'Lemoinei', 'Radiant' (w), 'Royalty', *M. scheideckeri*, 'Sissipuk' (w), 'Snowdrift' (w), and 'Vanguard'.

MORUS
MULBERRY

Value to birds: Fruit, shelter.

Used by: Bluebirds, cardinals, finches (house and purple), grosbeaks, mockingbirds, robins, thrashers.

Deciduous. In late spring and early summer, when blackberrylike fruits ripen, fallen fruits (and bird droppings) can stain pavement. Surface roots compete with other plants grown beneath the foliage. White mulberry (*M. alba*) and red mulberry (*M. rubra*) reach about 50 feet high with broadly rounded foliage canopies. Persian mulberry (*M. nigra*) grows to about 30 feet. Trees adapt to a wide range of soils and climates.

MYRICA
WAX MYRTLE

Value to birds: Fruit.

Used by: Cedar waxwings, flickers, robins, thrushes, towhees, warblers.

Evergreen. Pacific wax myrtle (*M. californica*) and southern wax myrtle (*M. cerifera*) form upright, shrubby trees to about 30 feet—neat if undramatic, with glossy, narrow leaves. Inconspicuous male and female flowers are borne on separate plants; in fall and winter, female plants carry waxy grayish purple berries.

PICEA
SPRUCE

Value to birds: Seeds, shelter.

Used by: Chickadees, creepers, finches (including siskins), grosbeaks, kinglets, nuthatches, waxwings, woodpeckers.

Evergreen. Seeds provide food, and needle-leafed branches offer year-round shelter. Unlike upright cones of firs, those of spruces are hanging. Many species are quite tall—rigidly upright, cone- or pyramid-shaped—but nurseries offer shorter selections, with needle color from dark green to silvery blue. Most spruces perform best in northern latitudes or higher altitudes.

PINUS
PINE

Value to birds: Seeds, shelter.

Used by: Cardinals, chickadees, crossbills, finches, flycatchers, hawks, jays, juncos, kinglets, nuthatches, owls, towhees, vireos, warblers, woodpeckers.

Evergreen. Widely adapted and grown, these cone-bearing, needle-leafed trees provide all-year bird shelter in all climates. Seeds ("pine nuts") in the cones are sought by many birds. Some pines mature at 30 to 40 feet, while others top out at over 100 feet. Growth in some is upright and narrow, in others rounded or irregular. Needles vary from 2 inches to more than a foot long, from stiff to almost limp. Select a species that offers dense foliage.

PRUNUS
CHERRY, PLUM

Value to birds: Fruit, shelter.

Used by: Bushtits (West), cardinals, cedar waxwings, finches, grosbeaks, jays, mockingbirds, quails, robins, sparrows, thrashers, thrushes, woodpeckers.

Deciduous and evergreen. Aside from cherries edible to humans, there are many other cherries and plums to grow strictly for birds' benefit. See the regional plant lists starting on page 81 for specific suggestions. Fruits of all cherries and plums can be messy if they fall on pavement. In spring, bare branches of deciduous kinds are covered with blossoms of white or pink. Red to purple (sometimes yellowish) fruits follow in summer, while autumn brings yellow, orange, or red foliage. Evergreen species offer purple to blue-black cherries on densely foliaged gigantic shrubs; spring flowers don't qualify as showy.

QUERCUS
OAK

Value to birds: Acorns, insects, shelter.

Used by: Bushtits (West), chickadees, finches, grosbeaks, hawks, jays, nuthatches, orioles, owls, titmice, towhees, vireos, warblers, woodpeckers, wrens.

Deciduous and evergreen. All oaks bear acorns—favored by many birds—though acorn (and tree) sizes and shapes vary greatly. Foliage canopies give good shelter and also harbor insects for additional food. Species include evergreen oaks for mild-climate gardens and deciduous ones for cold-winter regions. Native species, and those from climates similar to yours, usually are the best oaks to plant.

SASSAFRAS ALBIDUM
SASSAFRAS

Value to birds: Fruit, shelter.

Used by: Bluebirds, catbirds, robins, thrushes, vireos, woodpeckers.

Deciduous. Blue black berries in fall feed several bird species. Some trees are self-fertile or produce both male and female flowers—assuring fruit crop. Others bear male and female flowers separately, requiring both for the female tree to fruit. Fall foliage is orange, red, and copper.

SORBUS
MOUNTAIN ASH

Value to birds: Fruit, shelter.

Used by: Bluebirds, catbirds, cedar waxwings, grosbeaks, orioles, robins.

Deciduous. Clusters of small white flowers, showy berries (generally red), and colorful fall foliage offer changing interest. To birds, fruits are what count. A number of species are sold, all fairly fast growing. They tolerate heat and cold, partial shade or sun, and need summer moisture.

THUJA
ARBORVITAE

Value to birds: Seeds, shelter.

Used by: Mockingbirds, pine siskins, thrushes, warblers.

Evergreen. Small cones furnish seeds; evergreen, scalelike foliage gives winter shelter. *T. occidentalis*, a 40- to 60-foot tree, is less widely available than its shrubby forms. Best performance is in regions having moist atmosphere and soil; severe cold turns foliage brownish. Western red cedar (*T. plicata*) may reach 100 feet or higher.

TSUGA
HEMLOCK

Value to birds: Seeds, shelter.

Used by: Chickadees, finches, grosbeaks, jays, kinglets, nuthatches, thrushes.

Evergreen. Horizontal to drooping branches bear flattened, needlelike leaves; overall effect is dense and feathery. Small brown cones hang from the branches, providing eagerly consumed seeds. *T. canadensis* and *T. caroliniana* may reach 70 feet but can also be maintained as handsome clipped hedges.

Blossoms & Seeds

Although trees, shrubs, and vines are the basic plants you use to create a bird habitat, a number of annuals and perennials will also offer food to birds. Even weeds can contribute, if you'll tolerate the presence of a few.

Certain annuals, perennials, and weeds provide eagerly consumed seeds if their flowers are allowed to remain on the plant to set seeds. Many of these plants also harbor insects, which some birds eat. Petals are eaten, too. In the perennials list at right, some plants (marked *) also will attract hummingbirds to their blossoms for nectar.

Annuals. Any of the following common annual flowers yields a seed crop that will entice resident seed-eating birds: ageratum, amaranth, bachelor's button, calendula, China aster, coreopsis, cosmos, forget-me-not, marigold, Mexican sunflower, nasturtium, sea lavender, snapdragon, sunflower, sweet alyssum, and zinnia. Sunflowers, in fact, are such a favorite food source—and so bountiful in seeds (as well as easy to grow)—that you might want to grow a patch of them for harvest. Then you will have a quantity of seed to offer in feeders during winter and early spring (see pages 85–95).

Perennials. Showy flowering perennials include many plants that specifically appeal to hummingbirds for nectar—see page 79. For seed production, consider planting these: columbine*, coreopsis, foxglove*, purple coneflower, California poppy, gloriosa daisy, and goldenrod. Many of the ornamental grasses, such as *Pennisetum*, also provide a welcome seed crop in late summer and autumn.

Weeds. If you have an out-of-the-way patch where you can let weeds grow at will, you might encourage the annual wild grasses and grains. Among perennial weeds especially appreciated by some birds for their seeds are dock, fennel, and plantain.

Meadow blooms with poppies—golden orange California poppies, white and red Shirley poppies.

A Splashy Attraction

If your garden offers a water source that birds can use for drinking and bathing, you will greatly increase the number—and perhaps variety—of visiting and resident birds.

Design and placement. To entice birds to both drink and play, provide a gradual transition from very shallow to deeper water (but ideally no deeper than 3 inches). This might be a circular or rectangular structure where water deepens from edges to center; or it could have shallow and deep ends. The point is that a bird won't plunge into water of unknown depth but, instead, will wade into the water until it finds a depth to its liking. The steep-sided birdbath may attract drinkers, perched on its edges, but not bathers.

Be sure the bottom of the bath is not porcelain-smooth. Birds need a slightly rough-textured surface in order to maintain a good foothold.

A sure way to lure birds to a birdbath is to provide running water. At its simplest, this can be the frequent drip from a leaky faucet; grander schemes incorporate a fountainlike spray from garden sprinklers or small submersible pumps designed for garden pools. Drip-irrigation tubing and emitters make it easy to set up additions to your basic birdbath (for a do-it-yourself project, see page 108).

A bird wet from bathing can't move as fast as a dry bird, so it is important to place a birdbath near shrubbery where the bird can take cover from predators—but not so close to shrubs that predators can hide among them. A location about 10 to 20 feet from protective shrub cover offers a good "safety zone" for birds. If you're installing a ground-level birdbath, the space between bath and shrubs should be flat and open, giving predators no chance to creep up unnoticed. Avoid sites beneath overhanging tree branches or close to wood fences or flat-topped walls that could be launching pads for cats.

Upkeep. At the top of the birdbath care list is keeping the bath frequently refilled. An erratic water supply will draw fewer bird visitors. If your garden is watered by drip irrigation that is activated by an automatic controller ("timer"), you can place an emitter in the birdbath to fill it each time the watering system operates. Birds are attracted to clean water, so periodic cleansing of the water basin will keep the birdbath enticing.

In regions where birdbath water freezes, you'll need to work out a method for offering water throughout the winter. The old-fashioned method still works: use hot water from the house to melt birdbath ice. Or you can outfit your birdbath with a birdbath heater available from bird feed suppliers (see page 109). The simplest ones operate 24 hours a day; more expensive models incorporate a thermostat that shuts off the unit when temperature rises to a prescribed level.

Northern oriole sips at shallow, rocky garden pool.

Shrubs

Versatile shrubs can furnish varied layering in a birdscape, valuable for both food and protective cover, including nesting sites. Check pages 81–83 for the shrubs that do best where you live; hummingbird favorites are listed on page 79.

AMELANCHIER
SERVICEBERRY, SHADBLOW

Value to birds: Fruit.

Used by: Bluebirds, cedar waxwings, grosbeaks, phoebes, robins, towhees.

Deciduous. Summer crop of dark blue berries feeds a great variety of birds. These graceful, medium-sized to large shrubs are attractive in all seasons. White or blush flowers bloom in early spring; emerging foliage is pink, bronze red, or purple, maturing to green; in autumn, leaves change to yellow, orange, or red.

ARCTOSTAPHYLOS
MANZANITA

Value to birds: Blossoms, fruit, insects.

Used by: Bushtits (West), chickadees, jays, mockingbirds, quail, sparrows, thrashers, thrushes, towhees, wrens.

Evergreen. Tasty attractions for birds include blossoms in late winter, early spring; fruits (like pea-sized apples) in later spring or summer; and insects. Most manzanitas are Pacific coast natives successful only in that region. Many have good-looking branches of dark bronze to wine red; oval leaves of bright green to nearly blue gray; and small, clustered white or pink flowers. Most need well-drained soil, little or no summer water. Gardeners in Middle Atlantic, northern, and Pacific coast states use bearberry— *A. uva-ursi*—as low ground cover.

ARONIA
CHOKEBERRY

Value to birds: Fruit.

Used by: Bluebirds, catbirds, cedar waxwings, thrashers.

Deciduous. White or pinkish small flowers appear with leaves in spring. Fruits are red (in *A. arbutifolia*), purple (*A. prunifolia*), or black (*A. melanocarpa*); birds love them. Plants are fairly upright, spreading into clumps; red and purple chokeberries reach 10 feet, black no more than 5.

ATRIPLEX
SALTBUSH

Value to birds: Flowers, seeds, shelter.

Used by: Doves, finches, quail, sparrows, thrashers, towhees.

Evergreen and deciduous. Dense branches provide shelter and nesting sites; seeds and even flowers offer sustenance. Gray is the prevailing color of these desert and arid-region natives. Evergreen species range from 1 to 6 feet. Deciduous *A. lentiformis* forms a 10-foot mound of blue gray leaves on sometimes spiny stems. All saltbushes are drought-tolerant and fire-retardant, can be used as hedges.

BERBERIS
BARBERRY

Value to birds: Fruit, shelter.

Used by: Catbirds, cedar waxwings, mockingbirds, robins.

Evergreen and deciduous. Red, blue, or black fruits may be showy, but birds usually turn to them only after preferred berry sources have been stripped. The dense and usually thorny plants do offer popular shelter and nest sites. Hardiness varies, as do size and shape; all species are noted for toughness in a variety of climates and soils with ordinary care. Most have small but showy yellow or orange flowers, attractive small leaves; deciduous kinds offer bright autumn color change. Barberries make good impenetrable hedge plantings.

CALLICARPA
BEAUTYBERRY

Value to birds: Fruit.

Used by: Bobwhites, cardinals, catbirds, mockingbirds, robins, towhees.

Deciduous. Violet to purple autumn berries are both garden ornament and lure to birds. Spring flowers are inconspicuous on upright or arching 6- to 10-foot plants (depending on species). Stems may freeze to the ground in severe winters, but this does not stop fruit production: flowers (and then berries) are borne on new wood produced in spring.

Cotoneaster horizontalis

CORNUS
DOGWOOD

Value to birds: Food, shelter.

Used by: Bluebirds, cardinals, catbirds, grosbeaks, jays, robins, woodpeckers.

Deciduous. The shrubby dogwoods are less showy in flower than the tree dogwoods (see page 68), but the shrub species still attract birds with the same appealing berrylike fruits ripening from summer to fall. An insect population enhances the allure. Several species are widely sold, all forming upright clumps; all prefer moist soil. All have an autumn foliage show; some have colored stems. Those with bright red winter stems include Tatarian dogwood (*C. alba*), bloodtwig dogwood (*C. sanguinea*), and redtwig (or red-osier) dogwood (*C. stolonifera*), which spreads by underground stems into broad clumps. For coral red stems, choose Siberian dogwood (*C. alba* 'Sibirica'), a shorter plant to about 7 feet tall. *C. stolonifera* 'Flaviramea' is described by its common name, yellowtwig dogwood.

. . . Shrubs

COTONEASTER

Value to birds: Fruit, shelter.
Used by: Bluebirds, cedar waxwings, mockingbirds, robins, sparrows, thrushes.

Evergreen and deciduous. Small, applelike red fruits are a great ornament in fall and winter until birds find them. There are plants for nearly all climates, with varied growth habits: arching or simply bushy, low-spreading or ground-hugging. Most feature small white flowers in spring, followed by red, coral, or orange berries in autumn. All grow vigorously, even in rather poor soil.

ELAEAGNUS

Value to birds: Fruit, shelter.
Used by: Bluebirds, cardinals, grosbeaks, jays, mockingbirds, robins, thrushes, towhees, waxwings, wrens.

Evergreen and deciduous. Birds are lured by olivelike berries (red or brownish red), shelter, and nesting sites often protected by spiny stems. Inconspicuous but fragrant flowers come in fall on evergreen types; fruit matures in spring. Deciduous species flower in spring, the fruits ripening in late summer to autumn. Shrubs grow rapidly into dense, tough plants that tolerate heat, wind, indifferent soils. A silver cast suffuses foliage of all kinds.

EUONYMUS

Value to birds: Seeds, shelter.
Used by: Bluebirds, flickers, mockingbirds, sparrows, thrushes, warblers.

Deciduous and evergreen. In autumn, hanging seed capsules (variously shaped like miniature hatboxes or strawberries) turn orange, red, or yellow, then split open to reveal orange seeds. In deciduous species, this corresponds with flamboyant fall foliage. Tallest of deciduous kinds, *E. europaea*, reaches about 20 feet. Other species reach about 7 to 10 feet high.

HETEROMELES ARBUTIFOLIA
TOYON

Value to birds: Fruit, shelter.
Used by: Cedar waxwings, flickers, grosbeaks, mockingbirds, robins, thrashers, thrushes, titmice, towhees.

Evergreen. Its other name, California holly, describes this plant's fruits and its allure to varied birds. This dense shrub with glossy, dark green leaves can be kept at about 10 feet but will become a multi-trunked shrub-tree with little encouragement. Large clusters of tiny white flowers in late spring set small berries that ripen to brilliant red in late fall. Although drought-tolerant, toyon will accept summer moisture if soil is well-drained. Grow in sun or partial shade.

ILEX
HOLLY

Value to birds: Fruit, shelter.
Used by: Catbirds, cedar waxwings, mockingbirds, robins, thrashers, thrushes, towhees.

Evergreen and deciduous. Winter berries gladden numerous hungry birds. Although the most familiar hollies for festive decoration have red berries set against spine-edged, shiny green leaves, there are variations on this theme among the many holly species and varieties. There are hollies with smooth-edged leaves, hollies with variegated foliage, and some that lose their leaves entirely. Berries also can be yellow in selected varieties and black in several species. Nearly all are slow- to moderate-growers that form bulky, dense shrubs from knee-high to 20 feet or so. Evergreen kinds afford welcome winter shelter. The majority of hollies bear inconspicuous male and female flowers on separate plants, requiring a pollinating male plant for berry production. See *Ilex*, page 69, for details.

LIGUSTRUM
PRIVET

Value to birds: Fruit, shelter.
Used by: Bluebirds, cedar waxwings, finches, mockingbirds, sparrows, towhees, wrens (shelter for many birds).

Deciduous and evergreen. This classic hedge plant, if not formally sheared, will offer good shelter and nesting opportunities. (A closely clipped hedge will be too dense for bird entry.) Unsheared privets display tiny white blossoms in spring that later produce blue black, berrylike fruits to supplement birds' autumn and winter diets. All species thrive with little care in sun to partial shade and in any type of soil.

LINDERA BENZOIN
SPICE BUSH

Value to birds: Fruit, shelter.
Used by: Bluebirds, cardinals, catbirds, flickers, mockingbirds, robins, thrushes.

Deciduous. Dense, twiggy plants to 15 feet offer good shelter from spring leaf-out to autumn's blaze of golden foliage. Tiny, greenish yellow spring flowers that decorate bare branches mature to bright red ½-inch berries in early fall. To assure berries on a female plant, you need a male plant nearby.

LONICERA
HONEYSUCKLE

Value to birds: Food, shelter.
Used by: Cardinals, catbirds, chickadees, finches, robins, thrashers, towhees.

Deciduous and evergreen. Shrubby honeysuckles offer a varied bird banquet: succulent fruits, insects, and nectar-bearing flowers for hummingbirds. Fragrant blossoms are white or pink, produce small red or purple fruits that ripen in summer or autumn. Plants are arching or rounded, from 6 to 15 feet high. Two exceptions are evergreen box honeysuckle (*L. nitida*), an erect 6-footer, and semievergreen privet honeysuckle (*L. pileata*), with horizontal branches, to 4 feet high. All honeysuckle plants are vigorous and unfussy, thriving in many climates and soils.

MAHONIA

Value to birds: Fruit, shelter.
Used by: Cedar waxwings, mockingbirds, robins, towhees.

Evergreen. Handsome hollylike leaflets offer safe haven to birds in the dense-growing species, such as *M. aquifolium* (Oregon grape), *M. nevinii* (Nevin mahonia), *M. pinnata* (California holly grape), and *M. fremontii* (desert mahonia). Yellow spring flowers at branch tips are followed by usually blueberrylike fruits in summer and early autumn. Like the fruits of closely related *Berberis* (barberries), these are eaten by birds only after more favored fruits have been consumed. Numerous stems rise from the roots, branching to form a more spreading plant. All reach about 6 feet high—or can be maintained at that height.

MALUS SARGENTII
SARGENT CRABAPPLE

Value to birds: Food, shelter.

Used by: Cedar waxwings, grosbeaks, mockingbirds, robins.

Deciduous. This shrubby crabapple offers plentiful dark red fruits that appear in fall and last (if not eaten) into winter. Dense foliage and zigzag branching also offer good sanctuary. Lavish display of small white flowers in spring produces clusters of pea-sized fruits that ripen before leaves turn color; variety 'Rosea' has blossoms of pink. Rather slow growth eventually reaches about 10 feet high with a greater spread.

MYRICA PENSYLVANICA
BAYBERRY

Value to birds: Food, shelter.

Used by: Chickadees, finches, flickers, mockingbirds, robins, thrashers, thrushes, towhees.

Deciduous. After glossy, aromatic leaves change color and fall off in autumn, you clearly see the silvery, waxy berries that entice birds during winter. Compact shrub grows to about 9 feet—even in sandy, acid, nutrient-poor soil. Where winter cold is not severe, plants lose only part of their leaves. You need both male and female plants in order to get the bird-alluring fruits.

PHOTINIA

Value to birds: Fruit, shelter.

Used by: Cedar waxwings, finches, flickers, mockingbirds, quail, robins, thrashers.

Evergreen and deciduous. Like their relatives *Heteromeles* (toyon) and *Cotoneaster,* these plants display red berries (black when ripe in *P. glabra*) that ornament autumn and winter landscapes and attract birds. Large, dense shrubs, all have colorful new foliage and flattened clusters of white flowers in spring.

PRUNUS
CHERRY, PLUM

Value to birds: Food, shelter.

Used by: Cardinals, catbirds, finches, grosbeaks, jays, robins.

Deciduous. All furnish cherrylike fruits eagerly consumed by birds in summer. In addition to tree species (see *Prunus,* page 70), a number of strictly shrubby kinds exist—many native to North America and popular in regions of their origins. Spring brings a show of white or pinkish flowers on bare branches; summer offers red to purple or black fruits; autumn provides foliage color in yellow, orange, or red. Among nonnative species, good choices are Japanese bush cherry (*P. japonica*), growing 4 to 5 feet high, and Nanking cherry (*P. tomentosa*), which reaches 9 feet. Dwarf red-leaf plum (*P. cistena*) features purple leaves on a 6- to 10-foot plant.

PYRACANTHA
FIRETHORN

Value to birds: Fruit, shelter.

Used by: Bluebirds, cardinals, catbirds, cedar waxwings, finches, mockingbirds, robins, sparrows, thrashers, wrens.

Evergreen. Abundant autumn fruits are renowned for luring birds. In springtime, thorny branches are laden with clusters of white flowers against small, glossy leaves. In late summer or fall, branches blaze with pea-sized fruits of orange or red. Several species and many named varieties range from big, sprawling shrubs to low, spreading ground-cover types.

RHAMNUS
BUCKTHORN

Value to birds: Fruit, insects, shelter.

Used by: Finches, jays, mockingbirds, robins, sparrows, thrushes, towhees, wrens, wrentits (West).

Deciduous and evergreen. Birds consume the red to black fruits that appear in autumn and winter and are also attracted to a resident insect population. Spreading shrubs vary in height (depending on species) from about 12 to 20 feet or more; all buckthorns grow in sun to partial shade, are tolerant of less-than-regular watering.

RIBES
CURRANT, GOOSEBERRY

Value to birds: Flowers, fruit.

Used by: Bluebirds, catbirds, finches, flickers, robins, thrashers, towhees.

Deciduous. Summer fruits, generally red or black, are popular with birds, but blossoms also attract hummingbirds and some insectivores. Shrubs with thorns are gooseberries, while thornless-stem species are currants. Especially if armed with thorns, dense growth offers shelter to birds. Species native to North America are good choices in their regions. (Some are an alternate host to white pine blister rust and may be forbidden in certain areas.)

ROSA
ROSE

Value to birds: Fruit, shelter.

Used by: Cardinals, cedar waxwings, doves, grosbeaks, mockingbirds, quail, thrashers, thrushes, wrens.

Deciduous. Birds prefer species and shrub roses—any that produce a tangle of thorny stems and bear clusters of small fruits (called "hips"). Many native North American species fit these specifications, as does the Japanese native *R. multiflora.* Other suitable exotic species include the Scotch rose (*R. spinosissima*), Father Hugo's rose (*R. hugonis*), the sweet briar (*R. eglanteria*), the Austrian briar (*R. foetida*), and the species hybrid 'Harison's

Mourning dove nests in branches of rose (Rosa).

Conserving Your Crops

Gardeners who cultivate fruit crops soon make a vexing discovery—birds think they've been invited to a neighborhood potluck. As hungry guests, they're not particular: what's yours is theirs, too. Special favorites among fruit-eating birds are the cane berries (blackberries, raspberries, and their relatives—see *Rubus*, page 77), blueberries, cherries, grapes, and mulberries. But even larger fruits—apples, pears, plums, and figs—may be "sampled" just enough to disfigure or destroy part of the crop. Seed-eating birds can cut into a potential vegetable crop by consuming some of the newly planted seeds.

Through the years, frustrated gardeners have tried numerous humane methods to dissuade birds from marauding fruits and vegetables. These methods fall into three categories: protect, scare, and decoy.

Netting protection. The only totally effective way to save all of a crop is to cover it so birds can't get to it. Flexible nylon or vinyl-coated bird nettings, sold in rolls or large pieces, are easiest to use. You drape the material over the fruiting plant, and its small mesh (generally ½-inch) foils any attempts by birds to get to the fruits. Placed over a newly seeded vegetable garden, netting can remain on the soil until the seeds germinate. Agricultural supply stores, feed and grain stores, and even some hardware outlets carry bird nettings.

One drawback is that getting beneath the netting to harvest the crop can be a nuisance. Nettings are easiest to use on the shorter-growing plants, such as cane berries and blueberries; covering a full-sized cherry tree is something of a chore. However, any gardener handy with a hammer and nails can construct cage frames for specific crop plants, then cover the frames with bird netting or ½-inch-mesh poultry netting. Though this involves more work and cost, a cage can be designed so you can enter easily to harvest ripe fruits. The most useful designs are based on rectangular modules that can be assembled to protect a variety of plant sizes, then knocked down and stored when not needed.

Scaring devices. The old-fashioned scarecrow is one sort of device used to ward off birds by taking advantage of their sense of wariness. You can set out such a human effigy, or you can mount a stuffed replica of a hawk or similar predator in the crop tree. Around trees or smaller fruiting plants, you might stretch string from which you have hung objects that will flutter in the wind: shiny tin can tops, recycled aluminum packaging or strips of foil, jar lids, pieces of glass, streamers of bright or shiny fabric, or colored feathers. Noisy pinwheels or whirligigs mounted on stakes placed throughout a fruit planting are another scare tactic that has proven effective.

The problem with all fright methods is that birds quickly become accustomed to each device, realizing that it poses no real harm. For successful protection, you need to have a variety of methods ready to use so that you can change them every few days while the crop ripens.

Decoy fruits. The decoy principle operates on the theory that if you grow fruits that birds like best, they may leave most of your own preferred edible crop alone. To work at all, the decoy crop must ripen at the same time yours does, and it must be even more alluring to birds than what you're cultivating for your own table or canning jars.

Generally, birds appreciate a much more tart taste in fruits than do humans. Still, with sweet cane berries and blueberries as your cultivated crops, you may have little luck luring birds to other fruits—unless, perhaps, you plant a decoy mulberry (*Morus*). Decoy plantings of cane berries and blueberries can, though, divert birds from some of the larger fruits they could casually damage: apples, pears, and plums, for example.

. . . *Shrubs*

Yellow'. For the best range of choices among these bird-attracting roses, consult catalogs of mail-order suppliers offering old roses.

RUBUS
BRAMBLE

Value to birds: Fruit, shelter.

Used by: Cardinals, catbirds, grosbeaks, mockingbirds, quail, robins, sparrows, thrashers, vireos, warblers, wrens.

Deciduous. Brambles include all the popular cane berries—blackberry and raspberry, for example—as well as a few strictly ornamental plants. For a bird sanctuary, plant a berry patch and let it grow into a dense, somewhat unruly mound of interlaced canes. In this form, any of the brambles offers a good haven from predators in addition to luscious fruits in summer. Whenever your berry patch becomes too untidy or grows out of bounds, you can cut the canes to the ground and expect the planting to re-grow with vigorous new canes.

If you want a good-looking ornamental plant (but with fruits edible only by birds), look for Rocky Mountain thimble-berry *(R. deliciosus)*. Arching thornless branches to 5 feet high bear showy, single white flowers in spring followed by summer fruits.

SAMBUCUS
ELDERBERRY

Value to birds: Fruit, shelter.

Used by: Cardinals, cedar waxwings, flickers, grosbeaks, jays, mockingbirds.

Deciduous. Fast-growing elderberries reliably produce heavy crops of berries loved by birds. All species form large, bulky shrubs that can be severely pruned or cut to the ground whenever they become untidy. Large, flattish clusters of tiny white flowers form small red or blue-to-black berries that ripen in summer. Plants will thrive in continually moist soil but also tolerate considerable drought.

SHEPHERDIA
BUFFALOBERRY

Value to birds: Fruit, shelter.

Used by: Catbirds, flickers, grosbeaks, towhees, woodpeckers.

Deciduous. Clusters of small red berries give summer sustenance especially appreciated by birds in plains, mountain, and northern regions. Two North American species are cast-iron plants that thrive where frigid winters, hot summers, wind, and poor soil limit your landscape choices—*S. argentea* (silver buffaloberry) and *S. canadensis* (russet buffaloberry). In both species, inconspicuous male and female flowers are on separate plants; for fruit production, you need a male plant for pollination.

SYMPHORICARPOS
SNOWBERRY

Value to birds: Fruit, flowers.

Used by: Cedar waxwings, grosbeaks, robins, thrushes, towhees.

Deciduous. Showy fruits are useful to a bird's winter diet, but consumed only when tastier fare is exhausted. Several species are available, all making wispy plants that spread by suckers to form attractive thickets. Small spring flowers may attract hummingbirds; later these form large berries (white or purplish red, depending on species) on arching stems. All grow in sun or partial shade, with plentiful or little water.

VACCINIUM
BLUEBERRY, HUCKLEBERRY

Value to birds: Fruit, shelter.

Used by: Bluebirds, chickadees, flickers, robins, thrashers, thrushes, towhees.

Deciduous and evergreen. Birds and humans are equally fond of blueberries and huckleberries. If you plan pies, jam, or syrup, you'd better securely protect a few bushes (see page 76) for your own consumption. North America boasts numerous species, all of which need acid soil, regular moisture, and either sun or partial shade. *V. corymbosum* (highbush blueberry), the chief source of blueberries in the market, is particularly adapted to the Northeast and Northwest. In the Southeast, *V. ashei* (rabbiteye blueberry) is a better-adapted, similar plant. In western North America, *V. parvifolium* (deciduous red huckleberry) produces red summer fruits on a spreading or cascading plant. Another westerner, *V. ovatum* (evergreen huckleberry), is especially prized for its lustrous foliage—bronze at first, maturing to dark green.

Rubus (red raspberry)

VIBURNUM

Value to birds: Fruit, insects, shelter,

Used by: Bluebirds, cardinals, cedar waxwings, grosbeaks, mockingbirds, robins, sparrows, starlings, thrushes, towhees.

Deciduous and evergreen. A vast assortment of species and hybrids offers equal value to birds and gardeners. Most viburnums bear berrylike fruits (red, blue, or black, depending on species) in showy clusters that feed birds in autumn and winter. Evergreen *V. tinus* flowers in winter, bears blue fruits in summer. (Insects in spring and summer also supplement the diet.)

Most viburnums have handsome, dense foliage that offers good shelter. The deciduous kinds often give a brilliant fall foliage display of yellow, rusty gold, red, or purple. Fairly small spring flowers are white or pink, grouped in showy clusters; all will later bear fruits except the "snowball" types, which contain only sterile flowers.

Plant sizes range from several feet to shrub-tree proportions. Most are not particular about soil but need regular moisture for best appearance.

Vines

Lonicera (honeysuckle)

The tangled growth of climbing vines provides safe hideaways and nesting sites for birds. Vines also offer insects, nectar, fruits, and seeds. On the facing page, you'll find choices for attracting hummingbirds.

AMPELOPSIS BREVIPEDUNCULATA
BLUEBERRY CLIMBER

Value to birds: Fruit, shelter.
Used by: Bluebirds, catbirds, flickers, thrashers, thrushes.

Deciduous. Clusters of grapelike berries attract hungry birds in late summer and early fall. Greenish ivory when immature, berries ripen to a striking metallic blue. Vine is a rampant climber to 20 feet, needing support. In mild climates, large leaves turn red and drop in fall, but new leaves emerge green, changing to red throughout winter. Grow in sun or shade.

BERCHEMIA SCANDENS
SUPPLEJACK

Value to birds: Fruit.
Used by: Catbirds, mockingbirds, robins, thrashers.

Deciduous. Birds in the southeastern states frequent this native twining vine for its autumn clusters of small, blue black fruits. Handsome oblong leaves have distinctive parallel veins. A woodland native, it grows in sun or partial shade, reaching 15 to 20 feet.

CELASTRUS SCANDENS
AMERICAN BITTERSWEET

Value to birds: Fruit, shelter.
Used by: Bluebirds, cardinals, catbirds, cedar waxwings, robins.

Deciduous. In autumn, conspicuous yellow to orange seed capsules split open to reveal bright red seeds. Plants are either male or female; you need a nearby male plant to get fruits on the female. Light green oval leaves to 5 inches turn bright yellow in fall. Impressively vigorous, twining branches reach 20 feet or more, may need restraint to keep from overwhelming neighboring plants.

COCCULUS CAROLINUS
CAROLINA SNAILSEED

Value to birds: Fruit.
Used by: Bluebirds, mockingbirds, phoebes, robins, thrashers.

Deciduous. Showy small red fruits offer summer food to birds in this vine's native Southeast. Both male and female plants are needed for fruit production. Restrained growth twines to 12 feet, bearing broadly oval leaves.

EUONYMUS FORTUNEI 'VEGETUS'
BIG-LEAF WINTER CREEPER

Value to birds: Fruit, shelter.
Used by: Bluebirds, flickers, mockingbirds, thrushes.

Evergreen. *Euonymus fortunei* (winter creeper) encompasses vining, groundcover, and dual-purpose varieties. Best for birds, the big-leaf winter creeper offers an autumn crop of red seeds in orange capsules, also dense shelter from dark green leaves. It will grow as mounding shrub or attach itself to support (with assistance) as shrubby vine.

LONICERA
HONEYSUCKLE

Value to birds: Flowers, fruit, insects, shelter.
Used by: Catbirds, chickadees, finches, robins, thrushes.

Evergreen and deciduous. When established, these dense, twining vines give shelter. Fragrant flowers entice hummingbirds; red or black berries may follow in late summer and early autumn. Vigorous, evergreen Hall's honeysuckle (*L. japonica* 'Halliana') builds a tangled thatch of stems, bears white blossoms that age to chamois yellow. Similar, but much less rampant, is evergreen to semideciduous Henry honeysuckle (*L. henryi*). Flowers are yellow with red or purple shadings; fruit that follows is black. Red berries and yellow-orange to red unscented blossoms distinguish trumpet honeysuckle (*L. sempervirens*). Woodbine (*L. periclymenum*) bears fragrant creamy flowers opening from purple buds; berries are red—especially profuse in yellow-flowered variety 'Berries Jubilee'. Plants are evergreen where winter is mild, deciduous in colder regions.

PARTHENOCISSUS
BOSTON IVY, VIRGINIA CREEPER

Value to birds: Fruit, shelter.
Used by: Bluebirds, catbirds, chickadees, flickers, mockingbirds, robins.

Deciduous. To birds, these vines in autumn promise a crop of small, dark, grapelike fruits. *P. tricuspidata* (Boston ivy) gives dense cover; *P. quinquefolia* (Virginia creeper) has looser, more open growth. Their brilliant autumn foliage is legendary. Both vines are immensely vigorous when established, will thrive in sun or shade.

VITIS
GRAPE

Value to birds: Fruit, shelter.
Used by: Cardinals, finches, flycatchers, jays, mockingbirds, robins, thrashers, thrushes, towhees, vireos, warblers, wrens.

Deciduous. Grapes are as popular with birds as with humans. If a vine is allowed to scramble over other shrubs, it will form a tentlike bird refuge (at the expense of the host shrub). A thick vine trained over an arbor offers shelter and nesting sites. Grapes give an abundance of fruit clusters. Nearly all parts of North America have native or adapted kinds that benefit birds. All are far-reaching vines (without pruning) that climb by means of twining tendrils.

A Hummingbird Garden

Darting from flower to flower, its wings a blur of speed, the tiny hummingbird gathers nectar along with minute insects and spiders. (Shown above is a female Anna's hummingbird.)

Its rapid wing beats and almost ceaseless animation require extraordinary energy: a hummingbird must constantly refuel. In a day, one bird may consume more than half its weight in sugar.

Because hummingbirds feed from dawn to dusk, a garden full of their favorite flowers will attract and hold their attention. Along with hummingbird feeders (see pages 92 and 102), offer flowers at different levels (but not much lower than 18 inches): trees flanked by shrubs, bordered by perennials and annuals. Even on a small patio, you can place a favored vine against a fence, then plant annuals and perennials at its base and in containers.

In general, the most appealing flowers are trumpet-, funnel-, or tube-shaped and hold nectar at the blossom base. When you find hummingbirds visiting flowers that don't conform to those shapes, you can be sure that abundant nectar is the lure. Brightly colored flowers are best; red and orange are preferred, though blue and pink also are popular. The following generally attract hummingbirds.

TREES

Acacia
Albizia julibrissin (Silk tree)
Chilopsis linearis (Desert willow)
Citrus
Erythrina (Coral tree)
Eucalyptus
Liriodendron tulipifera (Tulip tree)
Melia azedarach (Chinaberry)

SHRUBS

Abelia
Abutilon (Flowering maple)
Buddleia (Butterfly bush)
Callistemon (Bottlebrush)
Cestrum (Night jessamine)
Chaenomeles (Flowering quince)
Correa (Australian fuchsia)
Erica (Heath)
Feijoa sellowiana (Pineapple guava)
Fuchsia
Grevillea
Hibiscus syriacus (Rose of Sharon)
Justicia (Shrimp plant, Brazilian plume flower)
Kolkwitzia (Beauty bush)
Lonicera (Honeysuckle)
Melaleuca
Ribes (Flowering currant)
Rosmarinus officinalis (Rosemary)
Weigela

VINES

Campsis radicans (Trumpet creeper)
Distictis buccinatoria (Blood-red trumpet vine)
Lonicera (Honeysuckle)
Pyrostegia venusta (Flame vine)
Tecomaria capensis (Cape honeysuckle)

PERENNIALS

Agave
Alcea rosea (Hollyhock)
Aloe
Alstroemeria
Anigozanthos flavidus (Kangaroo paw)
Aquilegia (Columbine)
Cuphea ignea (Cigar plant)
Delphinium
Digitalis (Foxglove)
Echium fastuosum (Pride of Madeira)
Gladiolus
Heuchera (Coral bells)
Impatiens
Ipomopsis aggregata
Ipomopsis rubra
Kniphofia (Red-hot poker)
Leonotis leonurus (Lion's tail)
Lobelia cardinalis (Cardinal flower)
Lobelia laxiflora
Lotus berthelotii (Parrot's beak)
Lychnis chaldedonica (Maltese cross)
Lychnis coronaria (Crown pink)
Mimulus (Monkey flower)
Mirabilis jalapa (Four o'clock)
Monarda (Bee balm)
Penstemon (Beard tongue)
Phlox
Phygelius capensis (Cape fuchsia)
Salvia (Sage)
Zauschneria (California fuchsia)

ANNUALS

Antirrhinum majus (Snapdragon)
Impatiens
Nicotiana (Flowering tobacco)
Petunia
Phlox drummondii (Annual phlox)
Salvia splendens (Scarlet sage)
Tropaeolum majus (Nasturtium)

Regional Plant Lists

Birds abound in all parts of North America where gardeners grow plants. But from one region to another, the bird population differs. Similarly, the selection of plants varies according to the particular characteristics of regional climates.

The trees, shrubs, and vines described on pages 68–78 represent plants known to attract birds and also likely to be attractive in the garden. Most of them have a fairly broad range of adaptability.

To help you choose which of these bird-attracting plants are best suited to your particular area, we have divided the United States into six broad climatic regions (see map below). Over the next three pages, you'll find listings of the tree and shrub species that perform best in each region. If, for example, you see that a species of *Abies* (fir) is

recommended for your area, read the general description for firs on page 68. (We limit the lists to trees and shrubs, as they form the backbone of a birdscape.)

Beyond this selection of plants are others of strictly regional use that will serve birds within more limited areas. Native plants of any region include bird-enticing species that grow almost solely within the confines of their native territory. Desert- and mountain-dwellers are especially aware of such plants. A well-stocked nursery that deals in natives can enrich your range of choices. Further suggestions may come from regional arboreta and botanic gardens; local Audubon Society chapters also may be able to suggest plants known to be bird favorites in your locale.

- Northeast
- Southeast
- Plains & Prairies
- Mountains, Great Basin & High Desert
- Northern Pacific Coast
- Southern Pacific Coast & Low Desert

Northeast

TREES

ABIES (Fir): *A. balsamea; A. concolor; A. homolepis*

ACER (Maple)

AMELANCHIER (Serviceberry, Shadblow)

BETULA (Birch): *B. lenta; B. papyrifera; B. populifolia*

CARPINUS (Hornbeam): *C. caroliniana*

CORNUS (Dogwood): *C. alternifolia; C. florida*

CRATAEGUS (Hawthorn): *C. crus-galli; C. laevigata; C. phaenopyrum*

ELAEAGNUS angustifolia (Russian olive)

ILEX (Holly): *I. decidua; I. opaca*

JUNIPERUS (Juniper): *J. chinensis; J. virginiana*

MALUS (Crabapple)

MORUS (Mulberry)

PICEA (Spruce): *P. engelmannii; P. glauca*

PINUS (Pine)

PRUNUS (Cherry, Plum): *P. cerasifera 'Allred', P. c. 'Atropurpurea'; P. padus; P. pensylvanica; P. serotina*

QUERCUS (Oak)

SASSAFRAS albidum (Sassafras)

SORBUS (Mountain ash): *S. alnifolia; S. aucuparia; S. decora*

THUJA (Arborvitae): *T. occidentalis; T. plicata*

TSUGA (Hemlock)

SHRUBS

AMELANCHIER (Serviceberry, Shadblow): *A. grandiflora; A. stolonifera*

ARONIA (Chokeberry)

BERBERIS (Barberry)

CORNUS (Dogwood): *C. alba; C. mas; C. racemosa; C. stolonifera*

COTONEASTER

ELAEAGNUS: *E. commutata; E. multiflora; E. umbellata*

EUONYMUS: *E. alata; E. americana; E. bungeana semipersistens; E. europaea*

ILEX (Holly): *I. glabra; I. laevigata; I. verticillata*

LIGUSTRUM (Privet): *L. amurense; L. ibolium; L. obtusifolium*

LINDERA benzoin (Spice bush)

LONICERA (Honeysuckle): *L. bella; L. maackii; L. morrowii; L. tatarica*

MALUS sargentii (Sargent crabapple)

MYRICA pensylvanica (Bayberry)

PYRACANTHA (Firethorn): *P. coccinea*

RHAMNUS (Buckthorn): *R. alnifolia; R. cathartica; R. frangula*

ROSA (Rose)

RUBUS (Bramble)

SAMBUCUS (Elderberry): *S. canadensis; S. pubens; S. racemosa*

SYMPHORICARPOS: *S. albus; S. chenaultii; S. orbiculatus*

VACCINIUM: *V. corymbosum; V. pallidum*

VIBURNUM

Southeast

TREES

ACER (Maple)

CARPINUS (Hornbeam): *C. caroliniana*

CELTIS (Hackberry): *C. laevigata*

CORNUS (Dogwood): *C. alternifolia; C. florida*

CRATAEGUS (Hawthorn): *C. crus-galli; C. laevigata; C. phaenopyrum*

ILEX (Holly): *I. aquifolium; I. cassine; I. decidua; I. opaca*

JUNIPERUS (Juniper): *J. chinensis; J. virginiana*

LIQUIDAMBAR styraciflua (American sweet gum)

MAGNOLIA: *M. grandiflora; M. virginiana*

MALUS (Crabapple)

MORUS (Mulberry)

MYRICA: *M. cerifera*

PINUS (Pine)

PRUNUS (Cherry, Plum): *P. caroliniana; P. cerasifera 'Allred', P. c. 'Atropurpurea'; P. padus; P. pensylvanica; P. serotina*

QUERCUS (Oak)

SASSAFRAS albidum (Sassafras)

SORBUS (Mountain ash): *S. alnifolia; S. aucuparia; S. decora*

TSUGA (Hemlock): *T. canadensis; T. caroliniana*

SHRUBS

AMELANCHIER (Serviceberry, Shadblow): *A. grandiflora; A. stolonifera*

ARONIA (Chokeberry)

BERBERIS (Barberry)

CALLICARPA (Beautyberry): *C. americana; C. bodinieri giraldii; C. japonica*

CORNUS (Dogwood): *C. alba; C. amomum; C. mas; C. racemosa; C. stolonifera*

COTONEASTER

ELAEAGNUS: *E. ebbingei; E. multiflora; E. pungens*

EUONYMUS: *E. alata; E. americana; E. bungeana semipersistens; E. europaea; E. kiautschovica*

ILEX (Holly)

LIGUSTRUM (Privet): *L. japonicum; L. ovalifolium; L. vulgare*

LINDERA benzoin (Spice bush)

LONICERA (Honeysuckle): *L. bella; L. fragrantissima; L. korolkowii; L. nitida; L. pileata*

MALUS (Sargent crabapple): *M. sargentii*

PHOTINIA: *P. glabra*

PYRACANTHA (Firethorn)

RHAMNUS (Buckthorn): *R. frangula*

ROSA (Rose)

RUBUS (Bramble)

SAMBUCUS (Elderberry): *S. canadensis; S. pubens; S. racemosa*

VACCINIUM: *V. ashei; V. stamineum*

VIBURNUM

For descriptions of trees, see pages 68–70. Shrubs are described on pages 73–77.

Plains & Prairies

TREES

ACER (Maple): *A. ginnala; A. negundo*

BETULA (Birch): *B. papyrifera*

CELTIS (Hackberry): *C. occidentalis; C. reticulata*

CRATAEGUS (Hawthorn): *C. succulenta; C. 'Toba'*

ELAEAGNUS angustifolia (Russian olive)

JUNIPERUS (Juniper): *J. scopulorum; J. virginiana*

MALUS (Crabapple)

MORUS (Mulberry): *M. alba; M. rubra*

PICEA (Spruce): *P. glauca; P. pungens*

PINUS (Pine)

PRUNUS (Cherry, Plum): *P. americana; P. pensylvanica; P. serotina*

QUERCUS (Oak): *Q. macrocarpa; Q. stellata*

SORBUS (Mountain ash): *S. aucuparia; S. decora*

THUJA (Arborvitae): *T. occidentalis*

SHRUBS

AMELANCHIER (Serviceberry, Shadblow): *A. alnifolia*

ARONIA (Chokeberry): *A. arbutifolia*

BERBERIS (Barberry)

CORNUS (Dogwood): *C. alba; C. stolonifera*

COTONEASTER

ELAEAGNUS: *E. commutata; E. umbellata*

EUONYMUS: *E. alata; E. europaea*

LIGUSTRUM (Privet): *L. amurense; L. obtusifolium*

LONICERA (Honeysuckle): *L. maackii; L. morrowii; L. tatarica*

PRUNUS (Cherry, Plum): *P. besseyi; P. cistena; P. japonica; P. tomentosa*

RHAMNUS: *R. cathartica; R. frangula*

RIBES (Currant, Gooseberry): *R. odoratum*

ROSA (Rose)

RUBUS (Bramble)

SAMBUCUS (Elderberry): *S. canadensis; S. pubens*

SHEPHERDIA (Buffaloberry): *S. argentea*

SYMPHORICARPOS: *S. albus; S. orbiculatus*

VIBURNUM

Mountains, Great Basin & High Desert

TREES

ABIES (Fir): *A. concolor; A. grandis; A. lasiocarpa*

ACER (Maple): *A. campestre; A. cappadocicum 'Rubrum'; A. ginnala; A. glabrum; A. negundo; A. tataricum*

ALNUS (Alder): *A. glutinosa; A. tenuifolia*

AMELANCHIER (Serviceberry, Shadblow): *A. canadensis; A. laevis*

BETULA (Birch): *B. pendula*

CELTIS (Hackberry): *C. occidentalis; C. reticulata*

CRATAEGUS (Hawthorn): *C. crus-galli; C. laevigata; C. lavallei; C. phaenopyrum*

ELAEAGNUS angustifolia (Russian olive)

JUNIPERUS (Juniper): *J. deppeana; J. occidentalis; J. osteosperma*

LARIX (Larch): *L. occidentalis*

MALUS (Crabapple)

MORUS (Mulberry): *M. alba; M. nigra*

PICEA (Spruce): *P. engelmannii; P. pungens*

PINUS (Pine)

PRUNUS (Cherry, Plum): *P. cerasifera 'Allred'; P. c. 'Atropurpurea'; P. maackii; P. padus*

QUERCUS (Oak): *Q. bicolor; Q. gambelii; Q. macrocarpa*

SORBUS (Mountain ash): *S. alnifolia; S. aucuparia*

TSUGA (Hemlock): *T. heterophylla*

SHRUBS

AMELANCHIER (Serviceberry, Shadblow): *A. alnifolia*

ARONIA (Chokeberry): *A. arbutifolia; A. melanocarpa*

ATRIPLEX (Saltbush): *A. canescens; A. hymenelytra*

BERBERIS (Barberry)

CORNUS (Dogwood): *C. alba; C. sanguinea; C. stolonifera*

COTONEASTER

ELAEAGNUS: *E. commutata; E. multiflora; E. umbellata*

EUONYMUS: *E. alata; E. europaea; E. kiautschovica*

LIGUSTRUM (Privet): *L. amurense; L. vulgare*

LONICERA (Honeysuckle): *L. fragrantissima; L. korolkowii; L. maackii; L. tatarica*

MALUS sargentii (Sargent crabapple)

PHOTINIA: *P. villosa*

PRUNUS (Cherry, Plum): *P. americana; P. besseyi; P. cistena; P. tomentosa; P. virginiana demissa*

RHAMNUS: *R. cathartica; R. frangula*

RIBES (Currant, Gooseberry): *R. aureum; R. odoratum*

ROSA (Rose)

RUBUS (Bramble)

SAMBUCUS (Elderberry): *S. canadensis; S. pubens; S. racemosa*

SHEPHERDIA (Buffaloberry): *S. argentea; S. canadensis*

SYMPHORICARPOS: *S. albus; S. chenaultii; S. orbiculatus*

VIBURNUM

For descriptions of trees, see pages 68–70. Shrubs are described on pages 73–77.

Northern Pacific Coast

TREES

ABIES (Fir): *A. amabilis; A. concolor; A nordmanniana; A. procera*

ACER (Maple)

ALNUS (Alder): *A. cordata; A. glutinosa; A. oregona; A. rhombifolia*

AMELANCHIER (Serviceberry, Shadblow): *A. canadensis; A. laevis*

BETULA (Birch): *B. pendula*

CARPINUS (Hornbeam): *C. betulus; C. caroliniana*

CORNUS (Dogwood): *C. controversa; C. florida; C. nuttallii*

CRATAEGUS (Hawthorn): *C. crus-galli; C. laevigata; C. phaenopyrum*

ILEX (Holly): *I. aquifolium; I. latifolia; I. opaca*

JUNIPERUS (Juniper)

LARIX (Larch): *L. decidua; L. kaempferi; L. occidentalis*

LIQUIDAMBAR styraciflua (American sweet gum)

MALUS (Crabapple)

MORUS (Mulberry): *M. alba; M. nigra*

MYRICA: *M. californica*

PICEA (Spruce): *P. engelmannii; P. pungens*

PINUS (Pine)

PRUNUS (Cherry, Plum): *P. cerasifera 'Allred'; P. c. 'Atropurpurea'; P. ilicifolia; P. lyonii*

QUERCUS (Oak): *Q. agrifolia; Q. chrysolepis; Q. douglasii; Q. garryana; Q. kelloggii*

SORBUS (Mountain ash): *S. alnifolia; S. aucuparia*

THUJA (Arborvitae): *T. plicata*

TSUGA (Hemlock): *T. heterophylla*

SHRUBS

AMELANCHIER (Serviceberry, Shadblow): *A. alnifolia*

ARCTOSTAPHYLOS (Manzanita)

BERBERIS (Barberry)

CORNUS (Dogwood): *C. alba; C. sanguinea; C. stolonifera*

COTONEASTER

ELAEAGNUS: *E. ebbingei; E. multiflora; E. pungens*

HETEROMELES (Toyon): *H. arbutifolia*

ILEX (Holly)

LIGUSTRUM (Privet): *L. japonicum; L. ovalifolium; L. vulgare*

LONICERA (Honeysuckle): *L. fragrantissima; L. korolkowii; L. tatarica*

MAHONIA: *M. aquifolium; M. pinnata*

MALUS sargentii (Sargent crabapple)

PHOTINIA: *P. fraseri; P. glabra; P. villosa*

PRUNUS (Cherry, Plum): *P. cistena*

PYRACANTHA (Firethorn)

RHAMNUS: *R. alaternus; R. californica; R. crocea*

RIBES (Currant, Gooseberry): *R. aureum; R. sanguineum*

ROSA (Rose)

RUBUS (Bramble)

SYMPHORICARPOS: *S. albus; S. chenaultii; S. orbiculatus*

VACCINIUM: *V. ovatum; V. parvifolium*

VIBURNUM

Southern Pacific Coast & Low Desert

TREES

ALNUS* (Alder): *A. cordata; A. glutinosa; A. rhombifolia*

BETULA* (Birch): *B. pendula*

CELTIS (Hackberry): *C. australis; C. occidentalis; C. sinensis*

JUNIPERUS (Juniper)

LIQUIDAMBAR styraciflua* (American sweet gum)

MAGNOLIA: *M. grandiflora*

MORUS (Mulberry): *M. alba; M. nigra*

MYRICA*: *M. californica*

PINUS (Pine)

PRUNUS (Cherry, Plum): *P. cerasifera 'Allred', P. c. 'Atropurpurea'; P. ilicifolia; P. lyonii*

QUERCUS (Oak): *Q. agrifolia; Q. chrysolepis*; Q. douglasii; Q. emoryi; Q. engelmannii*; Q. wislizenii**

SHRUBS

ARCTOSTAPHYLOS* (Manzanita)

ATRIPLEX (Saltbush): *A. canescens; A. hymenelytra; A. lentiformis*

COTONEASTER

ELAEAGNUS: *E. ebbingei; E. multiflora; E. pungens*

HETEROMELES arbutifolia (Toyon)

ILEX* (Holly)

LIGUSTRUM (Privet): *L. japonicum; L. ovalifolium; L. vulgare*

MAHONIA: *M. aquifolium; M. fremontii; M. nevinii; M. pinnata**

PHOTINIA: *P. fraseri; P. glabra*

PRUNUS (Cherry, Plum): *P. cistena*

PYRACANTHA (Firethorn)

RHAMNUS: *R. alaternus; R. californica; R. crocea ilicifolia*; R. frangula*

RIBES (Currant, Gooseberry): *R. aureum; R. sanguineum**

ROSA (Rose)

RUBUS (Bramble)

SYMPHORICARPOS: *S. albus; S. chenaultii; S. obriculatus*

VIBURNUM

(* = not grown in desert)

For descriptions of trees, see pages 68–70. Shrubs are described on pages 73–77.

A Wild Banquet

Supplemental feeding increases your garden's powers of attraction for the simple reason that nature usually can't match the concentrated supply of food you can provide. Birds often remember where they had a superb meal many months before, and they will return to the same spot for more.

Most people who keep feeding stations do so in the fall, winter, and early spring. Where winters get very cold, such feeders may offer birds the only food in the area. During spring and summer, feeding stations are less popular, probably because birds become territorial at these times of year and chase rivals away. And the seeds, berries, nuts, or insects available naturally in the growing season are more appetizing to birds than most supplemental foods. Many species that rely on seeds during the fall and winter shift to insects during the breeding season.

Whether a feathered clientele flocks to your feeders only seasonally or all year, catering a banquet for birds can give you great satisfaction. Birds bring beauty, music, and life to the garden, especially welcome attributes during the still, snowy winter months. And in harsh climates, you can be sure that you're doing the birds a real service by keeping feeders full and a birdbath free of ice.

Birds of a feather dine together when they discover a safe supply of food. These American goldfinches (see page 60) gather around for thistle seed.

Favorite Foods

What do our feathered friends like best to eat? Some, like finches and sparrows, depend mainly on seeds the year around. Blackbirds dominate a garden seed feeder during much of the year—but reject seeds during the nesting season, when a greater need for protein impels them to eat insects.

Insects are also the preferred diet of woodpeckers and warblers, but both will be attracted by a suet feeder as well. Even a piece of fruit occasionally entices these birds.

Although sunflower seeds appear to delight seed-eating birds almost anywhere, other seeds may vary in appeal from one locality to another. To find out what the birds in your neighborhood like best, experiment with small amounts of different seeds to see what disappears fastest. The following list of some backyard bird visitors and their preferred foods will also help. For further information on seeds, turn to pages 88–89; for recipes and feeding tips for nectar, suet cakes, and other favorite foods, see pages 92–93.

Remember that birds also need to drink—and bathe. Place a shallow, ground-level birdbath or 3-foot-high pedestal-type bath at a safe distance from any shrubbery where a cat could crouch—15 to 20 feet. Make sure the bath is within a quick flight's reach of overhead branches. (Also see page 72; for a birdbath to construct yourself, see pages 106–108.)

Doves are generally ground feeders that appreciate sunflower seeds, cracked corn, chicken scratch, and peanut hearts. To discourage these birds from overtaking smaller birds' feeders, provide their preferred feed on the ground or on a table feeder—or use feeders with small perches for the smaller birds.

Quail and other chickenlike birds can be attracted to feeder trays and ground-feeding areas. Try spreading chicken scratch near cover to attract them.

Hummingbird species that come to feeders at all are highly selective, partaking only at specialized hummingbird feeders that dispense sugar water (see recipe, page 92). Though present only during the nesting season in the northern states, in the Southwest some species may hover at feeders all year.

Woodpeckers are attracted primarily to suet as supplemental food, mainly in fall and winter.

(They're also occasionally interested in hummingbird feeders, fruit, and nutmeats.) Present suet in chunks or cakes; a mesh bag or wire cage attached to a tree trunk or post gives woodpeckers a place to cling while pecking at the suet inside.

Chickadees and titmice love sunflower seeds. Suet and peanut butter mixed with cornmeal (see pages 92–93), dispensed from suet logs and other feeders, also have strong appeal—especially in winter, when the birds need extra fat and protein to withstand the cold. Set out one or more very small feeders designed to stop competition from large birds.

Northern cardinals and other large finches prefer black oil sunflower seeds as well as safflower seeds, but they will dine on other seeds if their first choices are not available. These birds, present all year in most of their range, may approach ground feeders as well as raised trays and dispensers.

Dark-eyed juncos visit gardens mainly in winter. At first they are rather shy ground feeders, in the manner of many small sparrows. Mixed seeds attract them, and as they grow comfortable, they may alight on your deck or on a raised feeding tray.

Orioles, though shy at the feeder, still can be attracted in winter by fruit. Hang sections of apple, orange, or banana on a nail (see page 93), or offer grapes and small chunks of other fruit in a halved and hollowed-out coconut or grapefruit. These colorful visitors may also stop at the hummingbird feeder.

House and purple finches devour mixed seeds, with a preference for millet and sunflower. They will appreciatively feed on the ground, at a raised tray or table, or from a hanging seed dispenser.

Goldfinches and siskins may be drawn to sunflower or thistle (niger) seeds. Use a hanging mesh bag or tube feeder if offering the fine thistle seed.

Squirrels and chipmunks often raid backyard bird feeders. You can try diverting their attention to a feeder banquet all their own. Birdseed suppliers sell corn-on-the-cob, cracked corn, peanuts, and peanut hearts that appeal to squirrels; sunflower seeds are popular with squirrels, too.

Pests & Predators

When backyard feeders start to attract numerous and varied birds, pests and predators often show up soon afterward. This can lead to distressing incidents. One day you may find that a small feathered friend has been killed—or you may experience the frustration of losing quantities of birdseed to bullying pests.

Even if upsetting from a civilized perspective, the predator-prey relationship, as well as pesky thievery, is part of nature's balance and should not be strenuously controlled. Federal (as well as many state and local) laws forbid killing, trapping, or harassing hawks and owls, two common predators. But you can take benign steps to reduce any predator's or pest's advantage.

Outwit hawks, such as the American kestrel or sharp-shinned hawk, by placing feeders near dense cover into which birds can flee instantly.

If predators continue to threaten despite such measures, restrict feeding to the early morning, so birds will disperse before the hawks are up and about.

Guarding against cats—the most effective predators of ground-feeding birds—can be a real challenge. For the best protection, attach a small bell to your cat's collar, warning of its approach. Cyclone fencing around your yard, if secure at buildings and gates and flush with the ground, will block neighborhood cats. Remove such inviting means of access as overhanging tree branches. Low fencing can help in the immediate vicinity of ground-feeding birds. Cats will have to jump over it, giving birds just enough warning to escape.

Clear away dense shrubbery, which can hide cats, to a distance of 20 feet from feeders and birdbaths, leaving thorny shrubs, which keep cats out.

Pesky squirrels will often invade and conquer feeders. While no remedy is foolproof, it sometimes helps to provide squirrels with their own feeding station, offering peanuts, corn, and sunflower seeds; however, you do run the risk of attracting all their relatives.

You can also attach baffles underneath raised feeders. Available through mail-order catalogs and where bird-feeding supplies are sold, these collars of flared metal or plastic block the squirrel's access from below (see page 98). However, a feeder placed too close to a tree or fence may still be within reach of a jumping squirrel.

Backyard birders have devised imaginative ways to foil squirrels. These have proven to be effective:

■ Hang the feeder by heavy monofilament fishing line, difficult for a squirrel to navigate.

■ Suspend the feeder from a clothesline between pulleys, encasing the line with plastic pipe segments approximately 2 inches long. The pieces of pipe will spin when a squirrel lands on them.

■ Feed birds early in the day, and don't put out too large a portion. Birds will tend to clean out the feeder quickly, leaving nothing for squirrels.

Aggressive birds, such as pigeons, jays, starlings, house sparrows, and blackbirds, have acquired a bad reputation because of their habit of dominating feeders. Generally, the best way to turn away unwelcome bird species is simply to eliminate the kind of food that attracts them. Reduce the total amount of food put out, so that these birds must forage elsewhere for a satisfying diet. Small openings and perches on a feeder also thwart invasion by large birds.

To discourage pigeons, eliminate their favorite foods—cracked corn, chicken scratch, grains, and bread crumbs. Keep the ground under feeders clean.

If jays become a bother, try giving them their own feeding station, a good distance from other feeders, offering peanuts, nutmeats, and sunflower seeds.

If starlings and blackbirds encroach in great numbers, the only solution may be to stop all supplemental feeding temporarily. When you begin anew, put out limited portions in small feeders.

Birdseed & Other Supplements

To vegetarian birds, seeds are nutritious meals, conveniently packaged. The oil in seeds helps birds maintain enough fat on their bodies to sustain themselves during harsh winter weather while furnishing calories for their constant activity. Seed protein is also needed for birds' muscles, which work strenuously, especially in flight.

Seed-eating birds, such as grosbeaks, have heavy bills that can crack seed hulls. But some insectivores also eat seeds, especially when the insect supply is low. Lacking enough strength in the bill to crack a seed, an insectivore such as the chickadee holds the seed down with one foot, hammering with the bill to open it.

Once you start feeding birds, will they become dependent on your seed? Some believe that if you encourage migrating birds to stay through a severely cold winter by feeding them through the fall, they may perish if you suddenly stop feeding them. With the excellent survival skills of wild creatures, most lingering migrant birds would be able to forage from nearby feeders or other food sources if your supply ran out. Yet a severe snowstorm might be too much for them. If you don't plan to keep feeding through the winter, taper off the flow gradually, rather than cutting it off all at once.

Favorite seeds

Some kinds of seeds are more popular with birds than others; the following are the favorites. The chart on the facing page shows which birds are most attracted to each type of seed.

Although mixed birdseed is sold at many supermarkets and pet stores, it is usually more economical to buy separate kinds in bulk from a garden supplier, feed store, or Audubon center, or by mail order (see page 109 for sources).

Thistle (niger) seed. An import from Africa and Asia, thistle seed is also called "niger" seed; in no way does it resemble the familiar weed. A favorite of small finches, the tiny black seeds are often dispensed from a special mesh sock or tube feeder to prevent spillage. High in protein and fat, niger seeds offer the added value of not attracting squirrels or blackbirds.

Fresh and dried corn. Cracked corn appeals to smaller ground-feeding birds, but it has disadvantages. It rots quickly if it gets wet, and it attracts squirrels, pigeons, blackbirds, and house sparrows. On or off the cob, whole corn kernels (either fresh or dried) provide rich nourishment to larger birds.

Birdseed mix. Widely variable in composition, depending on commercial packagers and market fluctuations, seed mixes also vary in bird appeal and nutritional quality. They tend to include such unappealing but inexpensive grains as milo (grain sorghum), rice, oats, or wheat. (Starlings, often a nuisance in gardens, do love milo and hulled oats.) Avoid mixes with a reddish hue, which indicates too much milo; it will be wasted. Choose a mix that has a pale yellow cast, indicative of corn and millet.

White proso millet. Both red and white millet are available, but birds generally prefer the white type. Because of its hard seed coat, millet is less prone to swelling and rotting than other birdseeds, making it useful for hopper feeders as well as ground feeding.

Black oil sunflower seed. A fairly recent discovery as birdseed, black oil sunflower seeds are extremely popular. Their tiny size and thin hulls are easier for small birds to handle, and the seed is rich with oil.

Hulled sunflower seed. Attractive to smaller seedeaters, hulled sunflower seed leaves no mess to clean up under feeders—but it may rot in wet weather. Be sure to use feeders that discourage large birds.

Striped sunflower seed. As a birdseed, this has been used longer than other types. For birds with heavy bills, it's a popular, nutritionally rich food. Offer it unmixed, because sunflower seed–eating birds will just waste what you put with it.

Safflower seed. Best known as a food for cardinals, safflower seed offers a special advantage—gray squirrels usually leave it alone.

Shelled peanuts and peanut hearts. Both peanut hearts, removed during the process of making peanut butter, and whole, shelled peanuts will attract birds. Starlings prefer peanut hearts to all else, so beware if they're aggressive in your garden.

Peanuts in shell. Packed with protein and fat, peanuts in the shell may appeal to insectivores and seedeaters large enough to handle them. Jays and woodpeckers like this treat. String a few on a wire to hang from a tree limb.

Wintertime supplements

If your winter is severe, snow and ice may prevent birds from tapping all the natural resources they need. Supplement their backyard food supply by offering gravel, ash, crushed eggshell, and salt.

Certain birds, such as mourning doves and finches, require grit—tiny bits of stone, coarse sand, or crushed oyster shell—to crush seeds in their crops. You can purchase grit at feed and pet stores.

Ash (from the fireplace) or crushed eggshells will function as grit, too, while also replenishing minerals that birds may lack in a harsh winter. Coarse salt meets some birds' sodium needs.

Provide grit, ash, and salt on covered feeding trays or on the ground. Mix crushed eggshell with seed or suet.

A drink of water

Don't forget that seeds, peanuts, eggshells, and salt are sure to build up thirst in your feathered guests. Provide a birdbath, too (see page 72 for guidelines), making sure it's free of ice in winter. From specialty stores and mail order catalogs, you can buy heaters to keep the water in birdbaths from freezing.

Seed Preferences

	Thistle (niger) seed	Cracked corn	Mixed seed	White proso millet	Black oil sunflower seed	Hulled sunflower seed	Striped sunflower seed	Safflower seed	Shelled peanuts & hearts	Peanuts in shells
Northern bobwhite		■		■	■		■		■	
Mourning dove	■	■	■	■		■		■	■	
Woodpeckers					■		■		■	
Blue jay		■	■		■	■	■	■	■	■
Chickadees					■	■	■		■	
Tufted titmouse					■	■	■	■	■	
Northern cardinal		■	■	■	■	■	■	■		
Rufous-sided towhee	■	■	■	■	■	■	■		■	
Chipping sparrow	■		■	■	■	■				
Song sparrow	■	■	■	■	■	■	■		■	
White-crowned sparrow	■	■	■	■	■	■	■			
Dark-eyed junco	■	■	■	■	■	■	■		■	
Purple finch	■		■	■	■	■	■	■	■	
House finch	■		■	■	■	■	■		■	
Pine siskin	■		■	■	■	■	■		■	
American goldfinch	■			■	■	■	■			
Evening grosbeak		■	■	■	■	■	■	■	■	
House sparrow	■	■	■	■	■	■	■			

1. Thistle (niger) seed
2. Cracked corn
3. Mixed seed
4. White proso millet
5. Black oil sunflower seed
6. Hulled sunflower seed
7. Striped sunflower seed
8. Safflower seed
9. Shelled peanuts & hearts
10. Peanuts in shells

Tips for Success

Black-capped chickadees flutter outside a window before stopping for a snack of sunflower seeds. Feeder design prevents competition from larger birds.

What could be simpler than feeding birds? Just toss bread crumbs on the ground, and at least a few birds are bound to notice. But to really get a successful banquet going, follow these words of wisdom from seasoned backyard birders.

Keep a clean establishment

To help reduce chances of spreading avian diseases, maintain clean equipment and fresh food supplies.

■ Even if new, clean feeders thoroughly with mild soap and hot water before first setting them out.

■ Clean seed feeders again whenever they become wet and seed sticks to their corners.

■ Clean suet feeders often if the weather is warm enough to melt the suet or suet cake.

■ Change hummingbird nectar at least weekly in cool weather, twice a week in warm weather.

■ Clean any feeder when you suspect the food has spoiled or could make birds sick.

Feed in winter

Birds have the greatest need of your supplemental feeding in winter, especially if you live in a cold-weather region. Your feeding station will be the most useful if you follow these guidelines:

■ Set feeders on the south side of your house, if possible, to catch winter sun. Any moistened food will dry faster in sunlight, and dining birds will have to contend with less wind.

■ Set up feeders in September or October to attract birds as they first establish their winter feeding territories.

■ If you don't plan to feed all winter, cut down on seed gradually by about ¼ per week over a period of several weeks until the birds are less dependent on your feeding station.

■ Unless you plan to keep feeding through the warm season, gradually reduce feed and then remove feeders between March and May before birds become territorial in spring.

■ Set out feed if an unseasonable hard freeze occurs after you have stopped feeding. Continue feeding until natural food sources are available again.

■ Provide water for visiting birds, and be sure to keep it ice-free.

Provide protection

At feeders, birds are slightly less vigilant and more vulnerable than usual. You can protect your avian guests—and avoid losing seed because of weather conditions—by taking a number of precautions.

Place feeders within 20 feet of cover, but keep them a safe distance from low shrubs and ground cover where crouching cats could hide.

Don't position feeders where they might lure birds to fly into windows. Unfortunately, a reflection of the sky sometimes misguides a bird. Tight, fine netting in front of a window can help prevent calamity.

Use feeders with rooftops or other designs that protect seed from rain, snow, and garden sprinklers. Place them out of the wind to stop seed from blowing away and to protect birds from winter's chill. Keep suet out of direct sun, especially in warm weather, or it may go rancid.

The food supply

The following hints will help you to avoid problems that sometimes beset feeding stations.

■ Plan for how much food you wish (and can afford) to dispense per day. Within reason, birds will eat as much as you provide once a feeding station is established.

■ Feed early in the morning, when birds are the most active and are hungry for high-energy food.

■ Use seed mixes that have a high sunflower, corn, and millet content.

■ Mix peanut butter with cornmeal or other cereal to break its stickiness, which is believed to cause choking in birds. Use 1 part peanut butter and 4 to 6 parts meal.

■ Use the right feeders to avoid waste—thistle seed feeders for thistle seed, for example, and suet feeders for suet and suet cakes.

■ Choose feeders for small birds that will discourage invasion by larger birds and pests.

■ Avoid overfeeding; if you put out more than birds can eat in a single day, leftovers may attract squirrels, mice, rats, and unwanted bird species.

■ Put out only as much suet as birds can finish in a few days, or suet may turn rancid.

■ Don't let feed collect on the ground; rotting seed can cause disease and also result in weeds sprouting. Place feeders over decking or masonry for easiest cleanup.

■ If ants find the nectar feeder, hang it by a thin nylon fishing line. If the feeder attracts bees, coat openings with cooking oil, place in the shade, and keep outside surfaces of the feeder clean.

Beware of toxics

The safest and most welcoming backyard habitat for birds is an organically gardened area. To keep birds safe from chemical pollution, do not use insecticides, pesticides, fungicides, or herbicides while maintaining a feeding station. If you must spray, stop feeding at least a week before using toxic products. Use only biodegradable products, and spray late in the day. Do not resume feeding until past the contamination period specified on the label. Unless you've had rain since the spraying, water the garden well before you start feeding again.

Allow bird-feeder and birdhouse wood to weather naturally without potentially harmful stains, paints, or preservatives. Keep water fresh and clean.

Be patient

Attracting birds can become a great source of pleasure. But sometimes birds keep you waiting a long time. If your feeder is new, expect several weeks to pass before birds find it. They may return more promptly in subsequent years.

The first birds to show up will probably belong to the most common species for your area. Others will eventually notice the commotion and join in.

Don't give up until you have tried offering black oil sunflower seed, a favorite of many birds, or scattering scraps of day-old bread or doughnuts on the ground.

Mesh bag, originally used to sell oranges, makes a simple suet feeder accessible only to small, clinging birds.

Cakes & Other Snacks

Birdseed in its many forms is undoubtedly delicious to birds, judging by how quickly it disappears once your feeder is found. But birds will accept a variety of nourishment; preparing and even cooking occasional treats for them is an intriguing adventure. Even when you're offering everyday fare, a few preparatory steps in the kitchen can help prevent problems.

The recipes that follow are simple and quick enough for children to prepare. Watch your feeders to learn how well each culinary creation is received. You may see your feathered clientele expand in numbers and species as birds show up to sample the specialties of your house.

Stop weeds from sprouting from stray birdseed by cooking to prevent germination. Simply spread birdseed in a thin (about ¼-inch) layer on a cookie sheet with raised sides. Bake for 8 minutes in a 300° oven; cool completely before pouring into feeders. Baking sterilizes the seed, although it doesn't affect nutritional value.

You don't need to follow this procedure for thistle (niger) seed. Thistle, imported from Asia and Africa, has already been commercially sterilized by the time you buy it.

Hummingbird nectar for hummingbird feeders is a basic formula that you'll soon memorize if you cater to these tiny winged wonders. Keep in mind that the sugar water is valuable only to attract the birds, not as nourishment. Try to locate feeders near flowers that offer real nectar (for suggestions on what to grow, see page 79).

In a saucepan, combine 1 part granulated sugar and 4 parts water (⅓ cup sugar and 1⅓ cups water makes enough nectar to fill two standard satellite hummingbird feeders). Boil the mixture for 2 minutes, then allow to cool completely before using. After hummers discover and consume this formula, decrease the sugar proportion to 1 part to 6 (⅓ cup sugar to 2 cups water)—too much sugar can result in a liver dysfunction. The thinner solution will be safer and may encourage the birds to seek more natural food as well.

Store extra mix in the refrigerator for as long as several weeks. Do not use honey in place of sugar—it can cause bacterial and fungal infections in hummingbirds. Also, to prevent infection, thoroughly clean feeders at least once a week.

Peanut butter mix is popular with birds the year around. In cold winter weather, birds need the extra fat and protein peanut butter can provide. In summer, though their natural foods are much more abundant, insectivores still gain strength from a peanut butter mix during the demanding cycle of breeding and feeding their young. Don't offer peanut butter in hot weather, however, when it is prone to melting.

Birds can choke on peanut butter unless you mix it with another food to break up its sticky texture. Mix ½ cup smooth or crunchy-style peanut butter with 2½ cups cornmeal or uncooked oatmeal until well blended. If you wish, add about ¼ cup finely chopped leftover meat (in winter), dried fruit, or nutmeats. With a rubber spatula, apply thickly to a log feeder, such as the one on page 102.

Suet and suet cakes are another favorite winter treat that can be an important source of fat for birds in cold climates. Do not offer suet in warm weather, when it is likely to go rancid or melt, sticking to feathers.

Suet is hard beef fat—best from beef kidneys. You can buy it at meat markets, or just cut off the beef fat before cooking steaks or roasts at home. You can also purchase suet cakes from a bird-feeding supplier (see page 109 for listings). Cut the suet into chunks about 2 inches square and place in a mesh bag or other container, such as an inverted wire soap dish.

Rendered suet offers many possibilities (or offer rendered bacon fat instead). First cut the suet into small chunks, then melt it in a heavy pan over low heat or in a microwave oven. Pour the rendered suet into a small mold, such as an empty tuna can or a small muffin cup liner, and refrigerate it to harden; unmold before offering the cake to birds. Or pour rendered suet over a pinecone so that it fills every crevice; refrigerate to harden, then hang as a feeder.

To make suet cakes, mix slightly cooled rendered suet with other favorite bird foods: a tablespoon or two of peanut butter, cornmeal, oatmeal, chopped table scraps, dried fruits, or various birdseeds. For grit and calcium, mix in 1 or 2 well-crushed eggshells. Pour into paper-lined muffin cups. Refrigerate until hardened; then unmold and set out in a mesh bag or on a feeding table as cakes for birds. Watch to see which suet cake recipe appeals most to the birds in your garden.

Corn pudding, actually a rich version of suet cake, delights many birds and disappears quickly in cold weather. In a deep bowl, mix together 4 cups water and 2 cups sugar. In a heavy pan over low heat, slowly melt 2 cups suet or lard; allow to cool slightly, then stir into the sugar-water mixture, alternating with 4 cups yellow cornmeal, until a soft dough forms. Gradually stir in 4 cups all-purpose flour to make a stiff dough. Stuff dough deep into the crevices of large pinecones, then use string to hang the cones as feeders. You can also spread dough onto the log feeder shown on page 102.

Bird cakes make a hit with feathered friends for special occasions. Mix a cup of all-purpose flour with a cup of cornmeal, oatmeal, or bread crumbs, or a combination of the three. Moisten with ½ cup milk. Enrich with up to a cup of raisins, peanuts, or both combined. Also blend in ½ cup rendered suet, fat, or peanut butter. Bake in paper-lined muffin cups at 350° for 45 to 60 minutes, or until quite firm and brown. Cool, cut in sections, and present either on a feeder tray or in a mesh sack hung from a branch.

"Exotic" birdseed can be recycled from what you usually discard in the kitchen—fresh or dried seeds from pumpkins, other squashes, bell peppers, cucumbers, citrus fruit, papayas, pomegranates, and other fruits and vegetables. Save sesame, caraway, and poppy seeds along with crumbs from leftover baked goods. Add recycled seeds to any of the previous recipes. Sprinkle tiny seeds, such as caraway or poppy, on top of bird cakes before serving.

Fresh fruit entices orioles, tanagers, thrushes, and other shy garden visitors. Just hammer a nail an inch or two into a post or a thick board that can be hung on a tree trunk. (Make sure it is placed where no one will walk into it accidentally.) Impale half an orange or apple or a section of banana on the nail. A similar oriole fruit feeder is shown on page 98. Or place grapes, cherries, or any dried fruits on feeding trays; you might use a halved and hollowed-out grapefruit or orange as a container.

Coconut delight is fun for children to help prepare. Start by piercing the dark "eyes" in the top of a fresh coconut, using an ice pick, then drain the coconut milk. Place the coconut on a rimmed baking sheet and bake in a 350° oven for 15 minutes or until the shell starts to crack. Cool briefly, then break open by placing the coconut on a hard surface and striking it with a hammer. Fill the largest piece with crumbs of day-old bread, cake, or doughnut, or with fruit or nutmeats. Hang by a string from a tree limb or nail to a fence post.

Note: Use only fresh coconut to feed birds. Packaged coconut flakes have been known to harm birds by swelling inside them.

Appetizers, such as chunks of doughnut or stale poppyseed bagel, morsels of dog food, or finely chopped scraps of last night's dinner, may attract birds quickly—but don't offer these as a steady feeder diet. Birds will appreciate an opened pomegranate, too, but to avoid a mess offer it over a thicketed area.

Sunflower snacks appeal to many birds. To share their enjoyment, start by growing the giant flowers during the summer. When the flower heads dry in autumn (see below), birds will fly by to peck at the seeds. For bountiful flower heads, 8–10 inches across, grow 'Mammoth Russian' variety.

Delicious to birds and people alike are crunchy seeds from sunflowers.

A Birds' Christmas Tree

Cranberry garlands and suet stars taste like sugarplums to birds that fly near this snow-laden tree.

If you live in a climate of snowy winters, the Christmas season will be a time of year when birds especially appreciate your gift of edibles. Even where temperatures aren't freezing, decorating a Christmas tree for birds can be a fun way to celebrate the season.

Ideally, the tree you pick to decorate will be one you can watch from the breakfast table. Make sure that the tree is close enough to shrubs or other dense trees to offer cover if birds need to flee while snacking.

Delicious decorations

Preparing ornaments for a birds' Christmas tree is fun for both children and adults. Most of the kinds of bird feed mentioned earlier in this chapter can be adapted, with a little imagination, as decorations to hang on the tree.

Strings of popcorn, unbuttered and unsalted, will look festive on your tree—and taste like a holiday treat to birds. Use dark, heavy-duty thread, and pop enough corn to allow for breakage during stringing. To keep each kernel intact, poke a sharp needle through its puffy center.

Deck the popcorn garlands carefully over the tree's branches, tying ends with string to keep them from slipping or blowing off.

Cranberry and grape garlands add bright contrast to the popcorn. String packaged cranberries and fresh grapes on heavy-duty thread, adding nuggets of fresh apple and dried fruit, if you wish.

Oranges and grapefruit, cut in quarters, make delicious ornaments for birds. Tie pieces firmly to sturdy branches, fruit side up.

Corn-on-the-cob (either dried or fresh, uncooked) can be bound with string to strong inner branches.

Whole peanuts can be threaded to make a long garland, or you can hang a few from a short length of wire. String up large, shelled nutmeats as well.

Small pinecones become a special treat when dipped in rendered suet or stuffed with peanut butter mix (both explained on page 92). Dangle by looped string from the tree.

Christmas cookies for birds are fun to make, using the suet, peanut butter, and seed-cake recipes on pages 92–93. Harden the "cookies" by refrigerating in small molds. Add a few raisins for festive appeal.

Inviting the guests

Once the birds of your neighborhood have found your garden Christmas tree, they'll stay until the last morsel and berry have been consumed—provided a cat doesn't scare them off. But issuing an invitation can take a little time.

Do this by putting out some preferred birdseed, such as sunflower seed, close to the decorated tree. Even a handful of seeds broadcast on the ground or placed on a platform feeder can attract winter finches. Soon the reds, whites, and browns of purple and house finches, as well as the yellows, whites, and blacks of evening grosbeaks and perhaps even a bobwhite, may add their color to your tree.

Be sure, also, to offer a safe drink of water. Place a birdbath or small nonmetal pan of ice-free water near or under the tree if the area is safe from cats (otherwise, position it about 15 feet away). Read more about water for birds on page 72.

Christmas Bird Counts

Nearly a century ago, adhering to an old American tradition, outdoorsmen celebrated Christmas Day by shooting whatever wildlife came into sight. In 1900, a handful of bird-watchers challenged this violent custom and helped to replace it with the peaceful practice of counting birds. Today, volunteers all over the United States and beyond methodically count birds for the National Audubon Society during a two-week period before and after Christmas.

In this new holiday tradition, more than 1,550 separate bird counts are taken by bird-watchers from Barrow, Alaska, to Freeport, Texas, and from Newfoundland to the Farallon Islands off San Francisco Bay. Roughly 42,000 participants count birds from midnight to midnight of a 24-hour period in each specific area. Counts are held in every U.S. state and Canadian province, as well as in Central and South America as far as Brazil.

Why spend a day in wet and cold weather counting birds? Besides the chance of sighting an unusual bird, Christmas counters contribute to science and to the preservation of our natural environment. Scientists use Christmas bird count data to track the impact of tropical rain forest destruction on avian populations, for example, or the impact of rapid development on the islands of the Pacific.

Counts are not usually documented (except for rare species), because they cannot be exact—no one could see and count every last ruby-crowned kinglet in a given area, for example. But comparisons of counts taken in different years or weather conditions help to document local environmental concerns; they can influence decisions on park and community management for the benefit of birds. Ornithologists use the information to track such phenomena as the eastward expansion of house finches and other species. More generally, information is used to track avian population trends, range fluctuations, and winter species distribution.

Local backyard feeder reports add important portions of this data. Gardens and backyard feeders often attract the most unusual species seen on Christmas count lists.

To join the excitement, contact your local Audubon Society chapter or natural history association—your garden may or may not be inside one of the count circles for your state or province. Or write to the National Audubon Society, American Birds, 950 Third Avenue, New York, New York 10022.

As yet, no bird count of comparable size and organization has been established at any other time of year, although a breeding count in early summer is taken on a limited scale. Organizations such as the U.S. Fish & Wildlife Service and Cornell University's Laboratory of Ornithology do conduct less extensive counts of birds.

Purple finch, which actually looks rosy, perches conveniently for counting.

Feeders, Houses & Baths

To draw the flash of wings and the dash of bird song to your backyard, you'll need to provide prospective tenants with the three things they need most: food, shelter, and water. We've already discussed the principles of landscaping your backyard habitat; now it's time to get down to nuts and bolts.

If you choose, you can purchase a whole spectrum of attractive bird feeders, birdhouses, and birdbaths. But if you're at all handy with tools, you may want to build them yourself.

Most of the do-it-yourself projects we've selected are easy to put together using a few standard homeowners' tools—saw, measuring tape, brace and bit, and hammer—though you'll probably find that a portable circular saw and a power drill will make the work go more smoothly. A radial-arm saw and a table saw are great for crosscutting, ripping, and shaping the occasional bevel, but they aren't necessities. In many cases, you can substitute simple butt joints for trickier connections. If you're working with acrylic plastic, cut and drill it with standard woodworking tools, or order it cut to size.

Decay-resistant redwood, cedar, and cypress are best for wood feeders and houses, but use whatever scraps you have on hand. Don't bother to varnish, or even (unless the woodworker in you insists) to finish-sand: birds like their accommodations on the rough side.

Bird feeders and houses make ideal do-it-yourself projects, requiring only a minimum of tools, materials, and time. The redwood hopper feeder (foreground) is detailed on page 101; for birdhouse designs, see pages 103–105.

For Sale: Bed, Bath & Board

Most of this chapter features projects for do-it-yourselfers, but on these two pages we present a cross-section of commercially available feeders, houses, and baths. If you're all thumbs—or short on time—you'll find many choices at hobby and pet supply shops, nurseries, and nature stores. The mail-order sources listed on page 109 also offer a wide selection of birding products.

Eating out. When it comes to feeders, you can choose sleek acrylic, lightweight metal, or classic wood designs: the latter look especially at home in the garden.

Many birds relish black oil sunflower seeds. The tube-style feeder is a favorite way to offer these tiny seeds. If you want to attract goldfinches, put out a feeder designed specifically for their favorite food—niger (thistle) seed. For more on birds' preferences, see pages 88–89.

Certain feeders are designed for certain birds. For example, a satellite-type hanging feeder attracts small clinging species, such as chickadees and titmice. The weighted-perch model closes when a squirrel shows up but stays open when svelte birds arrive to feed.

Acrylic feeders that stick with suction cups to panes of glass are fun to watch but usually have limited seed capacity; most cater better to small birds than large. Cardinals may use this type of feeder, though they favor a flat surface rather than a perch.

A whole range of mounting poles, pivoting arms, and hangers awaits you in mail-order catalogs. Take steps to ward off thieves and predators: pest-resistant baffles and poles above or below the feeder help thwart industrious raccoons and squirrels (also see page 87).

Suet (solid beef fat) is a great treat for such insectivores as woodpeckers and mockingbirds, especially in winter when natural food is scarce and extra calories are needed. Special mesh or gridwork suet holders prevent greedy birds from making off with more than their share.

A fruit holder will attract visitors such as tanagers, orioles, and warblers.

Beating the housing shortage. It may come as a surprise, but birds can suffer from lack of shelter, particularly in recently developed suburban areas where gardens aren't mature enough to provide desirable nesting

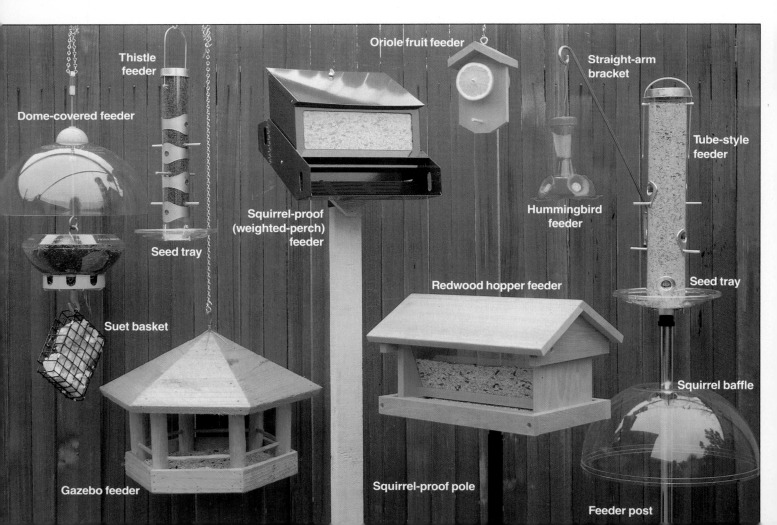

Dome-covered feeder

Thistle feeder

Oriole fruit feeder

Straight-arm bracket

Seed tray

Tube-style feeder

Squirrel-proof (weighted-perch) feeder

Hummingbird feeder

Suet basket

Redwood hopper feeder

Seed tray

Squirrel baffle

Gazebo feeder

Squirrel-proof pole

Feeder post

sites. Even rural farmland is not always hospitable; as woods are cut, brush cleared, and tree crops tended, the number of nesting areas is reduced.

Fortunately, man-made houses can provide a remedy. Wood is the old standby, and birds seem to feel cozy in a wood house, the rougher the better. Bird experts caution against paint—lead-based paints and some clear finishes may be toxic, and birds seem to shy away from those cute, colorful houses that most attract their human benefactors. Besides the gamut of wood styles and finishes, you can also find houses made of ceramic, metal, acrylic, and other materials. Aluminum purple martin houses are popular and much easier to hoist than their homemade wooden counterparts.

The most important consideration is that house dimensions, entrance hole, and mounting height be to the birds' liking. For guidelines, see the chart on page 104; also refer to the "How to attract" advice for many of the species in "A Garden Guest List," pages 21–61. These rules aren't cast in stone, but your odds are improved if you come close to following them. For mounting suggestions, see page 105.

Not all birds will use birdhouses—one good reason for knowing which birds frequent your part of the country. Nesting shelves, popular with swallows, robins, and phoebes, are designed to hang from a wall that is partially protected from both the elements and the watchful eyes of predators. These open structures offer a bonus—they let you observe the activities of your tenants.

Outdoor plumbing? As discussed on page 72, water in the garden is a powerful lure for birds. The vessel itself isn't critical, as long as it is very shallow, slopes gently, and has a rough surface. Beyond that, there's a large selection of ceramic, concrete, plastic, and even wooden birdbaths available.

Birds love water that gently drips or splashes. You can buy such birdbath accessories as fountain jets, drip spouts, and small portable heaters to thaw ice in winter. The submersible pump shown below, teamed up with some clear plastic tubing, recirculates water from a small garden pool to a fountain jet or waterfall, or through a pool filter. Spaghetti tubing and drip hardware are other gardeners' options for backyard waterworks.

Bluebird house

Chickadee house

Robin shelf

Wren house

Drip spout

Screech owl house

Wren house

Bracket-mounted bath

Purple martin apartment

Birdbath heater

Submersible pump

Terracotta pedestal bath

Ceramic "rock" pool

Catproof Feeder Tray

This platform feeder offers a tranquil dining room for hungry birds and keeps mischievous cats and scavenging squirrels at bay. The feeder hangs from a slippery 7-foot-tall pipe system braced by a 4 by 4 post.

Build the inner frame of 1 by 1s according to the drawing at right. Then nail on seven ½ by 4 slats to make the feeding platform (rip one of the slats lengthwise, if necessary, to make an accurate fit). Add 4 eyebolts as shown. Nail ½ by ½ strips for the food trap to the platform top. Finally, miter the 1 by 4s for the outer frame and nail in place.

Dig a hole for the 4-foot post and set it 2 feet into concrete. Assemble the pipe support, and attach it to the post with pipe clamps. Suspend the feeder from eyebolts with S-hooks and chain. Camouflage the pipe stand by planting honeysuckle at the base and training it up the pipe.

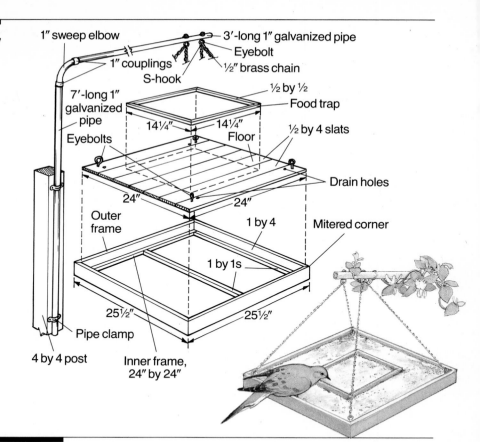

Homemade Hanging Feeder

Soggy seeds are the bane of many bird feeders, but this one has no such problem. It's fashioned from $3/32$-inch-mesh wire strainers—the kind you use in the kitchen.

If your strainers have large handles, cut them off. Make a hole for the center support rod by separating the wire mesh in the bottom of each strainer with a punch or large nail.

The load on the base of each strainer is spread out with 2-inch washers made from drilled-out lids from orange juice cans. (You could substitute another material.) To add support for larger birds, wrap pieces of $5/32$-inch aluminum clothesline around the rod and bend them up to the strainer's edge. Washers and nuts hold everything in place.

Drill a hole in the dowel perch just smaller than the threaded rod and twist to about 6 inches above the top strainer.

Design: Wally Doepel.

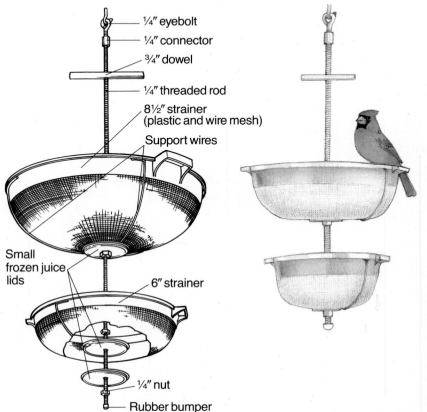

Classic Hopper Feeder

We show a fairly large feeder, but you can scale down all the dimensions if you like.

Cut rails, perches, floor, and side walls to size as shown. Drill ⅜-inch holes through perch rails; nail both sets of 1 by 2 rails to the floor. Insert dowel perches, adding a bit of waterproof glue to the holes. Sand off excess dowel.

Cut clear ⅛-inch acrylic into 7½- by 13-inch sheets (for best results, use a paneling blade on a portable circular saw or table saw). Add cleats to side walls, nail walls to base, then fasten acrylic in place with screws and finishing washers. Attach 16-inch-long roof pieces, hinging one side as shown.

Secure the barn to a length of galvanized steel pipe or a wooden post.

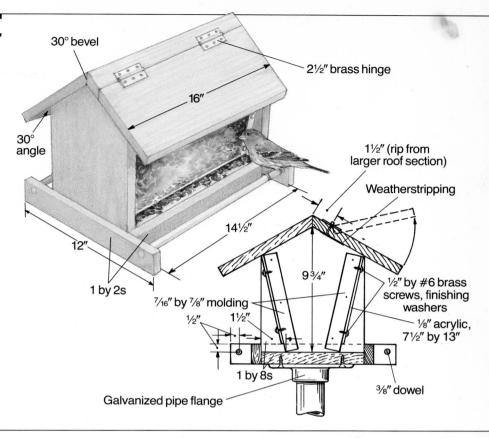

Thistle Feeder

Acrylic tubing is the key to this feeder, designed to please finches and other thistle fanciers. We used ⅛-inch-thick acrylic, cut 16 inches long, plus two plastic caps—the bottom one glued in place, the top one loose for refilling.

To locate acrylic, look in the Yellow Pages under "Plastics: Rods, Tubes, Sheets, Etc." Cut, drill, and sand the tube as required with standard woodworking tools. Seed "dispensers" are tiny, elongated openings—to make one, first drill a ¹⁄₁₆-inch hole, then let the drill "travel" a little up or down. Drill ¼-inch holes for dowel perches and smaller holes for a hanging wire.

Hammer dowels into place, then secure the bottom cap with slow-setting epoxy. Wire, brass chain, and an S-hook complete the hanging hardware.

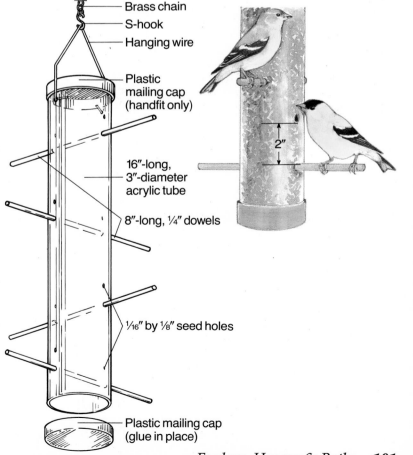

Hummer Feeder

Manic hummingbirds need a feeder all their own, filled with a solution of water and sugar (for details on making hummingbird nectar, see page 92).

Any bottle or jar, tipped at an angle and hung from a tree, eave, or special mounting bracket, can serve as a hummingbird feeder. For the fancier version shown at right, simply fit a bottle with a tight rubber stopper and bent glass tube. A little fishing around at either a pet store or a scientific supply outlet should turn up both stopper and tube. Hang the unit in a shady spot: rapid temperature changes cause hummingbird feeders to leak.

Hummers love red, so bright tape or an artificial red flower can help attract them. Once they know where the free nectar is, you probably won't need the color inducement.

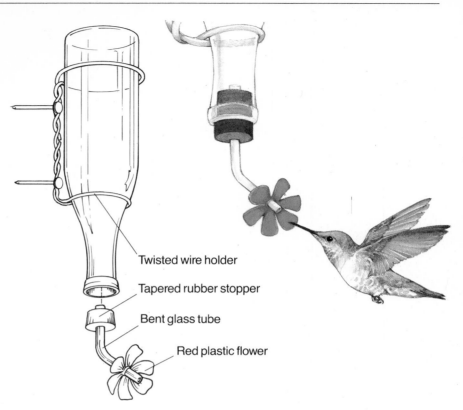

Twisted wire holder

Tapered rubber stopper

Bent glass tube

Red plastic flower

Simple Suet Feeders

Suet is a special winter treat for insect eaters such as woodpeckers. To keep big birds from carrying away more than their share, you can simply wrap suet with ½-inch wire mesh. String or mesh bags (the kind often used for oranges or onions) also make good containers. A tree-attached berry basket or wire-cage soap dish is another option. Feeling industrious? Try the tapered wooden feeder shown at right.

You can also make a suet feeder from a small log. Drill 1-inch-diameter holes into (but not through) the log, then fill with melted suet. Refrigerate to harden the suet, then hang the log from a tree limb. To attract birds that can't cling to tree trunks, insert small wooden dowel perches below some of the holes.

For an even quicker project, just dip a pinecone in melted suet to hang out for the birds.

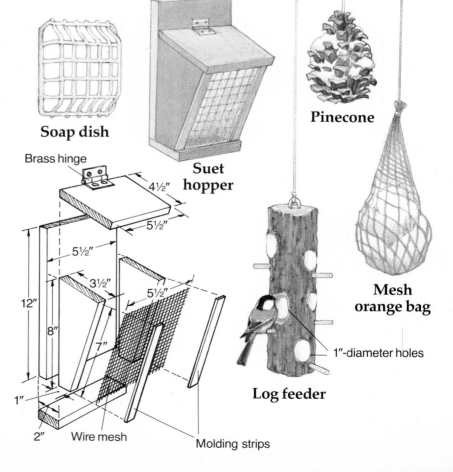

Soap dish

Suet hopper

Pinecone

Brass hinge

4½"

5½"

5½"

3½"

5½"

12"

8"

7"

1"

2"

Wire mesh

Molding strips

Log feeder

1"-diameter holes

Mesh orange bag

Nesting Shelves

Certain bird species—robins, phoebes, and barn swallows are good examples—prefer to nest on open platforms rather than in standard "box" houses.

The two shelf designs shown at right are easy to build: use any surfaced 1-by lumber you have on hand (decay-resistant redwood, cedar, or cypress will last the longest). Cut pieces to allow for the floor space and headroom shown on the chart on page 104.

Both these units were designed to hang below eaves or from a house wall that is partially protected from the elements—and from the eyes of potential predators. Robins are also fond of "hidden" nooks in ivy or other vines. Drill two slots near the top of the back wall of the assembled shelf, then slip the slots over nails or screws secured to house framing.

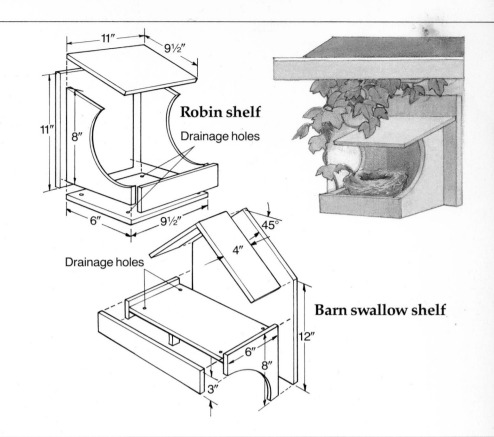

Robin shelf

Drainage holes

Drainage holes

Barn swallow shelf

Purple Martin Apartment

Purple martins are one of the few bird species that like to congregate with all their relatives; you'll need to provide an apartment house to attract them.

The structure should be lightweight, making it easy to raise and lower periodically for cleaning. It must also have good ventilation—purple martins take up residence for the whole hot summer.

The house shown at right is built from ½-inch exterior plywood and is roofed with asphalt composition shingles. A "ventilation shaft" effect improves air circulation on warm summer days. As your house catches on, you can easily expand upward—the design is modular.

Fill any edge gaps in each story with wood putty and sand smooth. Paint inside and out with white exterior latex to keep it cooler. Assemble with hooks and eyes, then mount to a stout pole or post, 15 to 20 feet high.

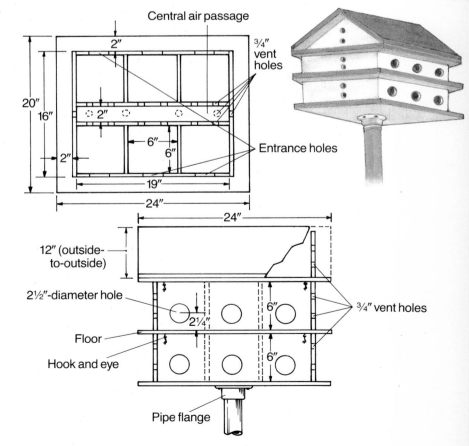

Central air passage

¾" vent holes

Entrance holes

12" (outside-to-outside)

2½"-diameter hole

Floor

Hook and eye

¾" vent holes

Pipe flange

Birdhouse Ideas

The answer to bird housing shortages—and a means by which to lure birds to your garden—is to offer man-made nesting structures.

Before you pick up a hammer and nails, become acquainted with some basic bird "building codes." Each species requires different accommodations. For example, a shoebox-size structure with a 2-inch hole won't attract the wrens that fly by. They simply won't use it; it's too large to be cozy, and the 2-inch opening will allow larger birds to enter and threaten the occupants.

The chart at right lists some familiar garden birds and gives specifications for their needs in house size, diameter of opening, and height of opening from the house floor. It also tells you how high above ground the house should be mounted.

Not all birds will use birdhouses. Swallows, for example, make their nests on open ledges, often just under the eaves of buildings. For ledge nesters, you need only provide a nesting shelf—for construction details, see page 103.

Keeping it simple. If you have even a passing acquaintance with a hammer and nails, you should be able to fashion a basic birdhouse like the one shown above right. Make it out of any ½-inch or 1-by (¾-inch) scrap lumber—decay-resistant woods such as redwood, cedar, and cypress are best. Simply rip (cut to width) and crosscut (cut to length) pieces with a handsaw or portable circular saw; drill the entrance hole with a brace and expansion bit, or use a power drill and spade bit or hole saw. The bevel (angle cut) shown where roof meets backing board makes the joint a little more seaworthy, but it isn't a necessity.

Simply nail the various pieces together, using galvanized box or finishing nails; hinge the roof as shown. Don't worry about the finish—birds don't care, and the house will weather, blending in with its surroundings. Nails are a quick and

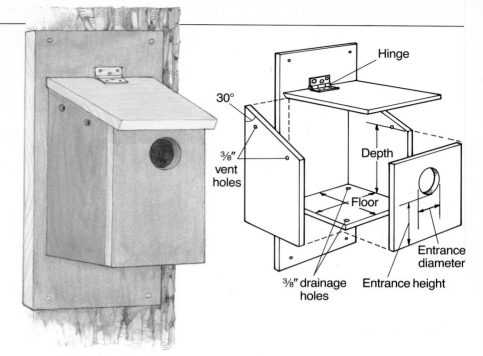

Basic birdhouse

Species	Floor of Cavity	Depth of Cavity	Entrance Above Floor	Diameter of Entrance	Height Above Ground
House wren	4" x 4"	6"–8"	4"–6"	1½"	6'–10'
Carolina wren	4" x 4"	6"–8"	4"–6"	1½"	6'–10'
Black-capped chickadee	4" x 4"	8"–10"	6"–8"	1⅛"	6'–15'
Tufted titmouse	4" x 4"	8"–10"	6"–8"	1¼"	6'–15'
Nuthatch	4" x 4"	8"–10"	6"–8"	1¼"	12'–20'
Bluebird	5" x 5"	8"	6"	1½"	5'–10'
House finch	6" x 6"	6"	4"	2"	8'–12'
Robin	6" x 8"	8"	*	*	6'–15'
Black or eastern phoebe	6" x 6"	6"	*	*	8'
Violet-green swallow	5" x 5"	6"–8"	4"–6"	1½"	10'–15'
Tree swallow	5" x 5"	6"–8"	4"–6"	1½"	10'–15'
Barn swallow	6" x 6"	6"	*	*	8'–12'
Purple martin	6" x 6"	6"	1"	2½"	15'–20'
Downy woodpecker	4" x 4"	8"–10"	6"–8"	1¼"	6'–20'
Hairy woodpecker	6" x 6"	12"–15"	9"–12"	1½"	12'–20'
Common flicker	7" x 7"	16"–18"	14"–16"	2½"	6'–20'
Red-headed woodpecker	6" x 6"	12"–15"	9"–12"	2"	12'–20'
Screech owl	8" x 8"	12"–15"	9"–12"	3"	10'–30'

*One or more sides open

easy mounting solution, but vinyl-coated wire (shown at bottom right) is kinder to your trees.

More advanced designs. Although the basic birdhouse works just fine as far as birds are concerned, the woodworker or landscaper in you may want to fashion something a little snazzier. One of the designs shown at right may fill the bill. Alter them or mix and match features as your mood dictates.

Although you can cut any bevels with a portable circular saw or saber saw, it's more accurate—and a lot faster—to use a table saw to rip and bevel all pieces. Cut the entrance hole with a hand brace with expansion bit, or a power drill with hole saw or spade bit.

The predator block shown on the birdhouse at center right is simply a scrap block of wood screwed to the inside of the front; the extra hole depth makes it tougher for outsiders to harrass the official tenants. Drill through both front and block at once. If you wish to fashion a drip cap, just cut a groove with a table saw's dado blade or use a portable router and straight bit.

Make connections with finishing nails (countersink them with a nailset) or decking screws (drive them with a power drill and Phillips head screwdriver bit).

Both these designs feature pivoting pieces that allow you access to the inside for seasonal cleaning. Form the pivot points by drilling through both fixed and moving pieces; then tap ⅜-inch dowels into the holes. The dowels are left loose (unglued), but they are sanded flush once installed. For best results, use a portable drill press or doweling jig to guide your drill bit. Secure the moving piece with a locking pin or screw as shown.

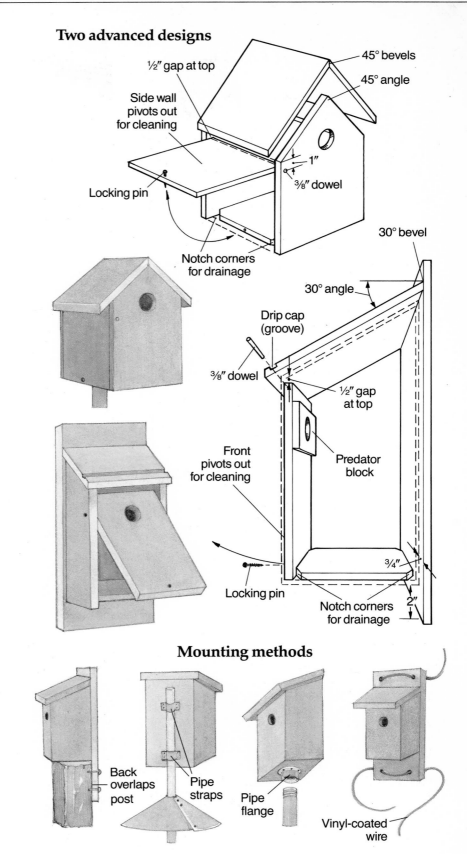

Two advanced designs

½" gap at top
Side wall pivots out for cleaning
Locking pin
45° bevels
45° angle
1"
⅜" dowel
Notch corners for drainage

30° bevel
30° angle
Drip cap (groove)
⅜" dowel
½" gap at top
Front pivots out for cleaning
Predator block
Locking pin
Notch corners for drainage
¾"
2"

Mounting methods

Back overlaps post
Pipe straps
Pipe flange
Vinyl-coated wire

Bamboo Waterspout

The sound of running water is a powerful attractor for birds, and this traditional water spout—or *tsukubai* in Japanese—is a simple way to provide it. Team up the spout with the concrete pool shown below, or use a rock with a natural hollow or some other type of small collecting basin.

It's easy to hollow out bamboo for use as piping: just ram a metal rod through it to puncture the joints. Then run flexible tubing through and connect the tubing to a drip system or faucet. Set the water flow at a very slow trickle. Channel any overflow to irrigate nearby plants or run into a larger pond.

To conserve moisture, hook up the system to a tiny pump on a timer or turn on a ball valve (see facing page) at certain times of the day. Early morning and late afternoon are times when birds are most active.

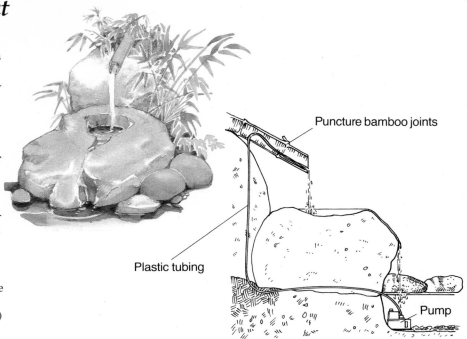

Puncture bamboo joints

Plastic tubing

Pump

Concrete "Rock" Pool

A small hand-packed concrete pool is the simplest type of natural pool for the do-it-yourselfer to build.

First, excavate and tamp the site, allowing for pool depth plus about 3 inches of concrete. In areas of freezing weather, dig down an extra 3 to 4 inches for a layer of gravel under the concrete. Add either chicken wire or welded steel mesh; bend it to shape, then prop it up with bits of rock.

Pack a very stiff concrete mix around the reinforcing, then finish the surface with a wood float or even a paintbrush; a "rough" finish provides footing for birds and allows moss and other plantings to take hold. To enhance the natural appearance, cover the walls with a mosaic of rocks set in mortar.

Give your new "rock" pool two coats of a commercial, cement-based waterproofing compound. Then cover and moist-cure the concrete shell for several days before use.

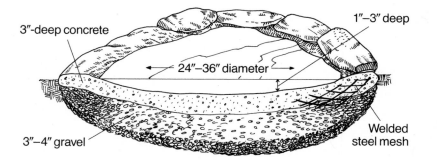

3"-deep concrete

1"–3" deep

24"–36" diameter

3"–4" gravel

Welded steel mesh

Waterfall & Pool

Nothing attracts birds to your garden like the sound of moving water. A small waterfall with reflecting pool like the one at right is usually a hit with humans, too.

Flexible liners are the big news in garden pools, and you'll find some type of liner in most garden centers and in virtually every mail-order garden-pool catalog (see page 109). These stout sheets—20 to 30 mils or thicker—are designed especially for garden pools. To figure liner size, add twice the pool's depth to its width, then tack on an extra 2 feet; repeat this procedure to find the correct length. In other words: liner size = $2d + w + 2$ *ft* by $2d + l + 2$ *ft*.

Liner installation is straightforward. Dig a hole to the contours you wish, adding 2 inches to the depth all around for a layer of sand. Level the excavation and add fine, damp sand, smoothing it with a wood float or steel trowel.

Drape the liner over the hole, weight the edges, and slowly fill with water while smoothing the liner into shape. Trim away all but about 6 inches of excess liner all around the pool and finish the edges with plants, rocks, flagstones, or some other material. Shallow water—from 1 to 3 inches deep—is best for birds; in deeper areas, be sure to furnish some rocks or a branch for birds to land on.

To add a waterfall, build up a foundation from rubble, sandbags, or the dirt excavated when you dug your pool. Lay down a strip of flexible liner on this foundation and solvent-weld it to the pool liner. Now place your primary rocks at the borders of the channel, being careful not to damage the liner. Add loose rocks or pebbles for visual accent or to form ripple patterns. To secure border plantings, pack soil behind the boulders.

A simple submersible pump recirculates water to the waterfall through flexible tubing. Power the pump with a GFCI-protected outdoor outlet; a ball valve controls the flow.

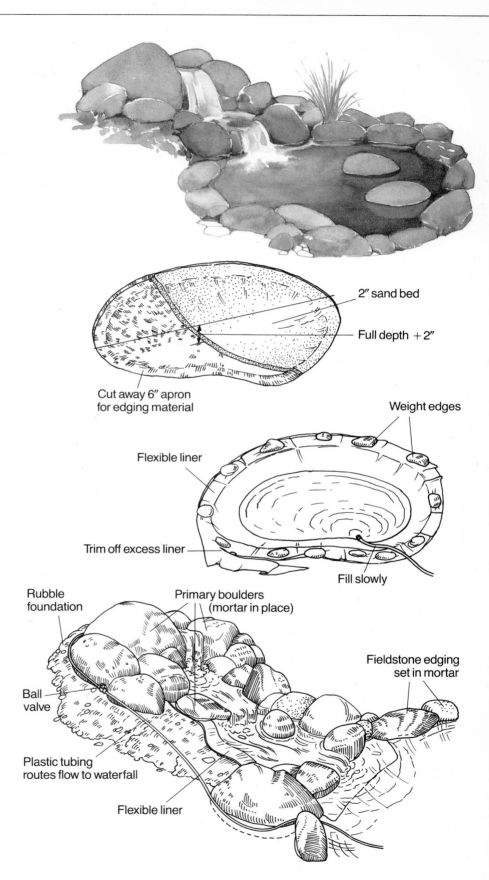

2" sand bed

Full depth + 2"

Cut away 6" apron for edging material

Weight edges

Flexible liner

Trim off excess liner

Fill slowly

Rubble foundation

Primary boulders (mortar in place)

Fieldstone edging set in mortar

Ball valve

Plastic tubing routes flow to waterfall

Flexible liner

Pedestal Birdbath

A sand-cast birdbath is not only great for thirsty, hygienic-minded birds, but it makes a custom garden accent as well.

To make a mold for the bath, dig a shallow hole, spread out wet sand, then drive a metal rod or pipe into the center as a pivot point. Construct a simple template like the one shown and fasten to a piece of PVC pipe to use as a swivel. Pivot the template to shape the sand mold, then touch up the sand with a wood float.

Now remove the template and pour a stiff concrete mix into the middle of the mold. Trowel from center to edge in one direction only, so sand is not disturbed, until the entire mold is covered with a 1-inch layer of concrete. Then bend welded steel mesh to the shape of the mold and press it into the concrete.

Pour another 1-inch layer of concrete over the reinforcing. Use your template to smooth the bowl, then fine-tune with a wood float (don't make the interior too smooth—birds won't like it). Smooth edges, cut the top off the pivot rod, and patch the hole before concrete sets.

Let your bowl damp-cure for 7 days, then mount on a large stump or post as shown.

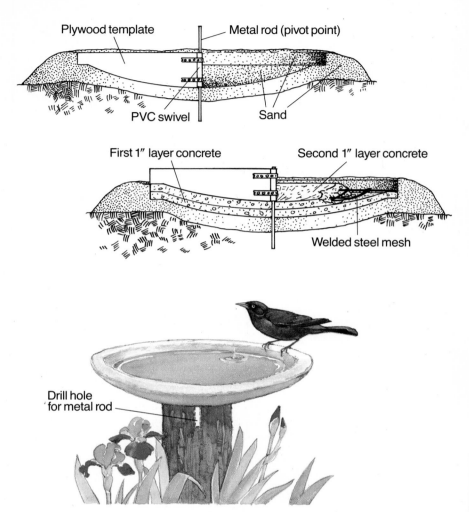

A Hot Tub for Birds

No, it's not really a hot tub—it's simply a redwood frame surrounding a recessed bath, plus a pair of hardwood perches for drinking and lounging.

Use a shallow plastic basin, photographic tray, or similar vessel to hold the water—just be sure it's not more than 3 inches deep and isn't too slick. Make the inner frame from construction-grade redwood or cedar; size it just large enough for the basin—but not the rim—to slip inside. Cut and drill the wider end panels as shown, then add ⅜-inch dowel perches.

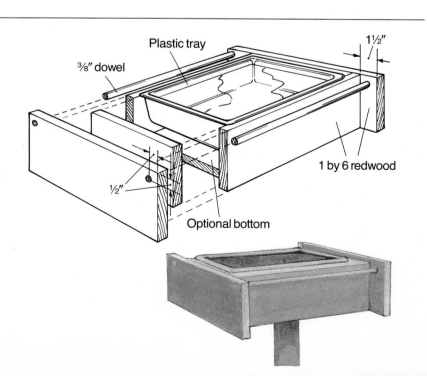

To Learn More . . .

If you want to find out more about bird-watching, bird feeding, backyard habitats, local birding clubs, and other subjects discussed in this book, the following organizations and publications can provide information.

Birding and conservation organizations:

American Birding Association, Inc.
P.O. Box 6599
Colorado Springs, CO 80934

American Ornithologists' Union
National Museum of Natural History
Smithsonian Institute
Washington, DC 20560

Cornell University
Laboratory of Ornithology
159 Sapsucker Woods Road
Ithaca, New York 14850

National Audubon Society
950 Third Avenue
New York, New York 10022
(Write for addresses of local branches.)

National Audubon Society
International Department
801 Pennsylvania Avenue SE
Suite 301
Washington, DC 20036

National Wildlife Federation
Backyard Wildlife Habitat Program
1400 Sixteenth Street NW
Washington, DC 20036-2266
(Kits are available for landscaping a habitat.)

The Nature Conservancy
1785 Massachusetts Avenue NW
Washington, DC 20036

North American Bluebird Association
P.O. Box 6295
Silver Spring, Maryland 20906

U.S. Fish and Wildlife Service
Department of the Interior
Washington, DC 20240
(Write for map of National Wildlife Refuges.)

Field guides:

Field Guide to the Birds of North America
Shirley L. Scott, Editor
National Geographic Society, Washington, DC

The Peterson Field Guide Series
Roger Tory Peterson
Houghton Mifflin Company, Boston
(Regional and beginner's guides are available, also CDs and cassettes of bird songs.)

Birds of North America
Chandler S. Robbins, Bertel Bruun, and Herbert S. Zim
Golden Press, New York

Familiar Birds of North America,
  Audubon Society Pocket Guides
Ann H. Whitman, Editor
Alfred A. Knopf, Inc., New York
(Regional editions are available.)

Catalogs of bird-feeding and garden pool suppliers:

Audubon Workshop
1501 Paddock Drive
Northbrook, Illinois 60062

BackYard Birds & Co.
717 S. Broadview Drive
Springfield, Missouri 65804

The Bird House
Box 722
Estacada, Oregon 97023

Bird 'n Hand
40 Pearl Street
Framingham, Massachusetts 01701

Droll Yankees Inc.
Mill Road
Foster, Rhode Island 02825

Duncraft
Penacook, New Hampshire 03303

Hyde Bird Feeder Company
P.O. Box 168
Waltham, Massachusetts 02254

Lilypons Water Gardens
P.O. Box 10
Lilypons, Maryland 21717

Van Ness Water Gardens
2460 Euclid Avenue
Upland, CA 91786

Wild Bird Company
617 Hungerford Drive
Rockville, Maryland 20850

Wild Bird Supplies
4825 Oak Street
Crystal Lake, Illinois 60012

Wild Birds Unlimited
1430 Broad Ripple Avenue
Indianapolis, Indiana 46220

Backyard Checklist

Listed below, in taxonomic order, are the 80 birds described in "A Garden Guest List," on pages 21–61. Record sightings of any of these species. If you see a particular bird in late April one year, you may want to watch for it at the same time in future years.

Date

Hawks
_____ American Kestrel

Gamebirds
_____ Ring-necked Pheasant
_____ Northern Bobwhite
_____ Gambel's Quail

Plovers
_____ Killdeer

Doves
_____ Rock Dove
_____ Mourning Dove

Owls
_____ Eastern Screech Owl
_____ Western Screech Owl
_____ Great Horned Owl

Swifts & Hummingbirds
_____ Chimney Swift
_____ Ruby-throated Hummingbird
_____ Black-chinned Hummingbird
_____ Anna's Hummingbird
_____ Broad-tailed Hummingbird

Kingfishers
_____ Belted Kingfisher

Woodpeckers
_____ Red-headed Woodpecker
_____ Red-bellied Woodpecker
_____ Yellow-bellied Sapsucker
_____ Downy Woodpecker
_____ Hairy Woodpecker
_____ Northern Flicker

Flycatchers
_____ Black Phoebe
_____ Eastern Phoebe

Swallows
_____ Purple Martin
_____ Tree Swallow
_____ Violet-green Swallow
_____ Barn Swallow

Date

Crows, Magpies & Jays
_____ Steller's Jay
_____ Blue Jay
_____ Scrub Jay
_____ American Crow

Titmice & Chickadees
_____ Black-capped Chickadee
_____ Carolina Chickadee
_____ Tufted Titmouse

Bushtits
_____ Bushtit

Nuthatches
_____ Red-breasted Nuthatch
_____ White-breasted Nuthatch

Creepers
_____ Brown Creeper

Wren
_____ Carolina Wren
_____ House Wren

Kinglets
_____ Golden-crowned Kinglet
_____ Ruby-crowned Kinglet

Bluebirds
_____ Eastern Bluebird
_____ Western Bluebird
_____ Mountain Bluebird

Thrushes
_____ Wood Thrush
_____ American Robin

Mimic Thrushes
_____ Gray Catbird
_____ Northern Mockingbird
_____ Brown Thrasher

Waxwings
_____ Cedar Waxwing

Starlings
_____ European Starling

Date

Vireos
_____ Red-eyed Vireo

Warblers
_____ Yellow Warbler
_____ Pine Warbler

Tanagers
_____ Scarlet Tanager
_____ Western Tanager

Grosbeaks
_____ Northern Cardinal
_____ Rose-breasted Grosbeak
_____ Black-headed Grosbeak

Buntings
_____ Indigo Bunting
_____ Painted Bunting

Sparrows
_____ Rufous-sided Towhee
_____ American Tree Sparrow
_____ Chipping Sparrow
_____ Song Sparrow
_____ White-throated Sparrow
_____ White-crowned Sparrow
_____ Dark-eyed Junco

Blackbirds
_____ Red-winged Blackbird
_____ Eastern Meladowlark
_____ Western Meadowlark
_____ Common Grackle
_____ Brown-headed Cowbird
_____ Northern Oriole

Finches
_____ Purple Finch
_____ House Finch
_____ Pine Siskin
_____ American Goldfinch
_____ Evening Grosbeak

Weavers
_____ House Sparrow

Index

Photographers

George K. Bryce/Animals Animals: 32 bottom; **Gay Bumgarner/Photo/Nats:** 35 top, 36 top, 72; **John Cancalosi/Tom Stack & Associates:** 23 bottom; **M. A. Chappell/Animals Animals:** 34 bottom; **Glenn Christiansen:** 75; **Mary Clay/Tom Stack & Associates:** 35 bottom, 36 bottom, 37 top, 41 bottom, 45 top, 56 top; **Priscilla Connell/Photo/Nats:** 24 top, 26 top, 27 top, 29 bottom, 30 top, 31 top, 38 bottom, 41 top, 43 top; **W. Perry Conway/Tom Stack & Associates:** 23 top, 57 top; **E. R. Degginger/Animals Animals:** 84; **Tom Edwards/Animals Animals:** 56 bottom; **Bill Everitt/Tom Stack & Associates:** 24 bottom; **Derek Fell:** 78; **Jeff Foott/Tom Stack & Associates:** 22 bottom; **John Gerlach/Animals Animals:** 20; **John Gerlach/Tom Stack & Associates:** 39 bottom, 43 bottom; **Warren Greene/VIREO:** 6; **C. H. Greenewalt/VIREO:** 27 bottom; **Wm. D. Griffin, Photography/Animals Animals:** 61 bottom; **George H. Harrison:** 58 top, 60 top; **Valerie Hodgson/Photo/Nats:** 53 bottom, 59 bottom, 91; **Thomas Kitchin/Tom Stack & Associates:** 25 bottom, 29 top, 30 bottom, 44 top; **Sid Lipschutz/VIREO:** 49 top; **Joe McDonald/Animals Animals:** 51 bottom; **Ells Marugg:** 68; **Brian Milne/Animals Animals:** 61 top; **Alan G. Nelson/Tom Stack & Associates:** 40 bottom, 50 top; **Don Normark:** 15; **John F. O'Connor, M.D./Photo/Nats:** 12, 25 top, 49 bottom; **Herbert B. Parsons/Photo/Nats:** 44 bottom, 46 bottom, 47 bottom, 57 bottom; **Don and Esther Phillips/Tom Stack & Associates:** 32 top, 37 bottom, 47 top; **Rod Planck/Tom Stack & Associates:** 40 top, 54 bottom; **Norman A. Plate:** 89; **C. R. Sams II and J. F. Stoick/VIREO:** 60 bottom; **F. K. Schleicher/VIREO:** 31 bottom; **B. Schorre/VIREO:** 1, 28 top, 52 bottom; **Stan Schroeder/Animals Animals:** 38 top; **G. W. Schwartz/Animals Animals:** 50 bottom; **Wendy Shattil, Robert Rozinski/Tom Stack & Associates:** 28 bottom; **John Shaw/Tom Stack & Associates:** 34 top, 48 top, 54 top; **Robert C. Simpson/Tom Stack & Associates:** 22 top, 33 top, 42, 45 bottom, 48 bottom, 51 top, 52 top, 53 top, 55, 58 bottom; **Michael Thompson:** 71, 73; **John Trott/Animals Animals:** 62; **T. J. Ulrich/VIREO:** 33 bottom; **Darrow M. Watt:** 93; **Jack Wilburn/Animals Animals:** 39 top, 46 top; **J. R. Woodward/VIREO:** 59 top, 95; **Tom Wyatt:** 77, 96, 98, 99; **D. & M. Zimmerman/VIREO:** 26 bottom.